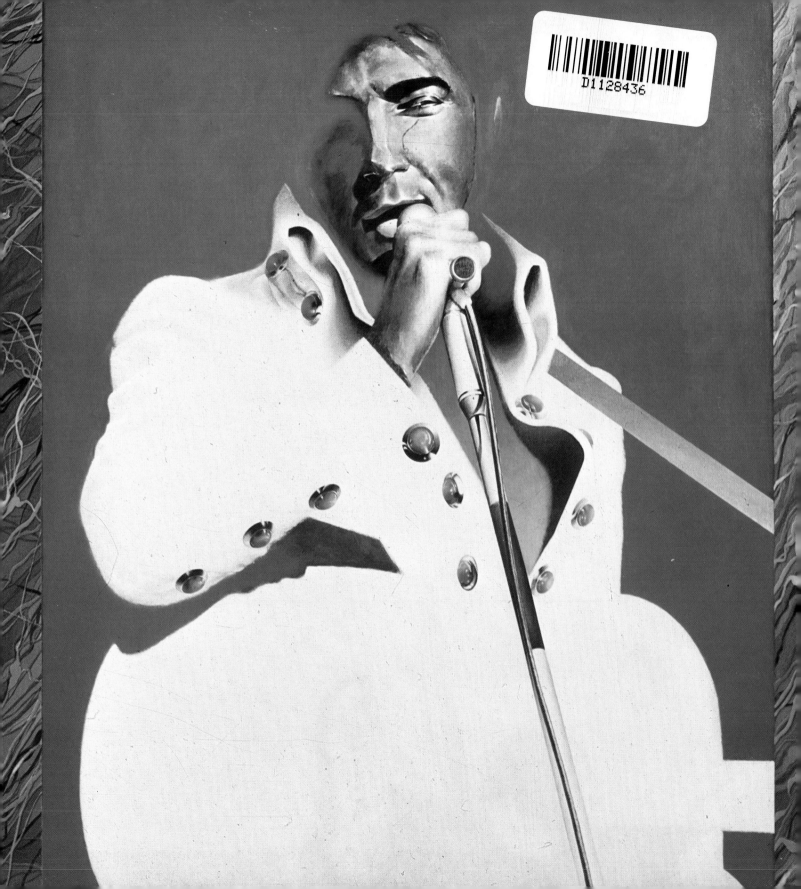

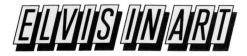

ELVIS IN ART

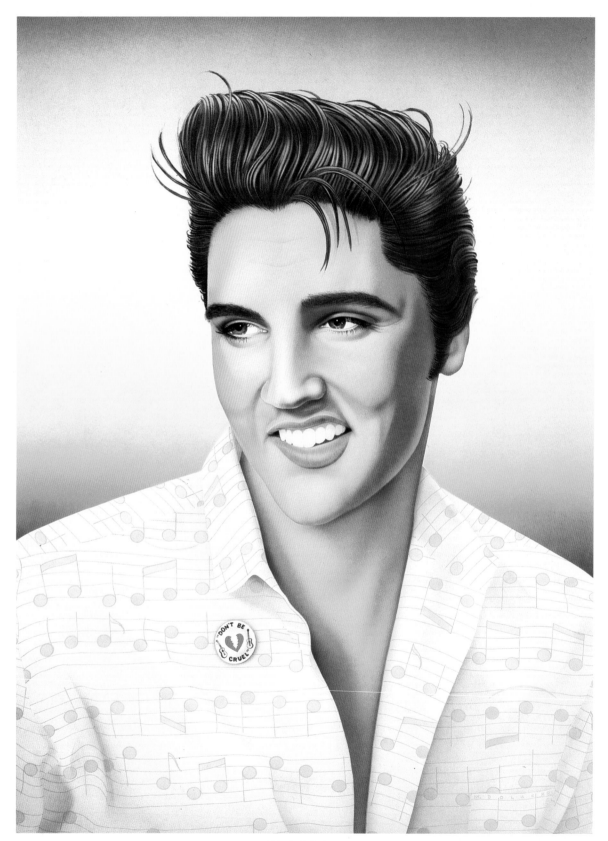

Monte Dolack

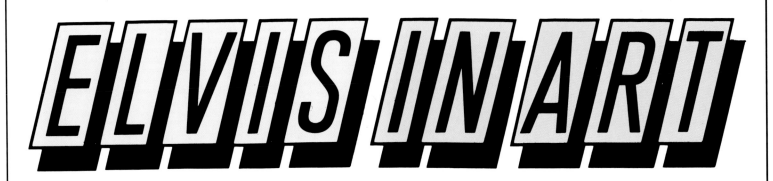

ELVIS IN ART

COMPILED BY ROGER G. TAYLOR

St. Martin's Press/New York

For Pip and Max

Elvis in Art
Introduction and collection copyright © 1987 by Roger Taylor

Design by Craig Dodd

ISBN 0-312-01381-7

First edition

10 9 8 7 6 5 4 3 2 1

First published in 1987 in the United Kingdom by
Elm Tree Books/Hamish Hamilton Ltd

Printed in Spain by Cayfosa Barcelona.
Dep. Legal: B-24559-1987

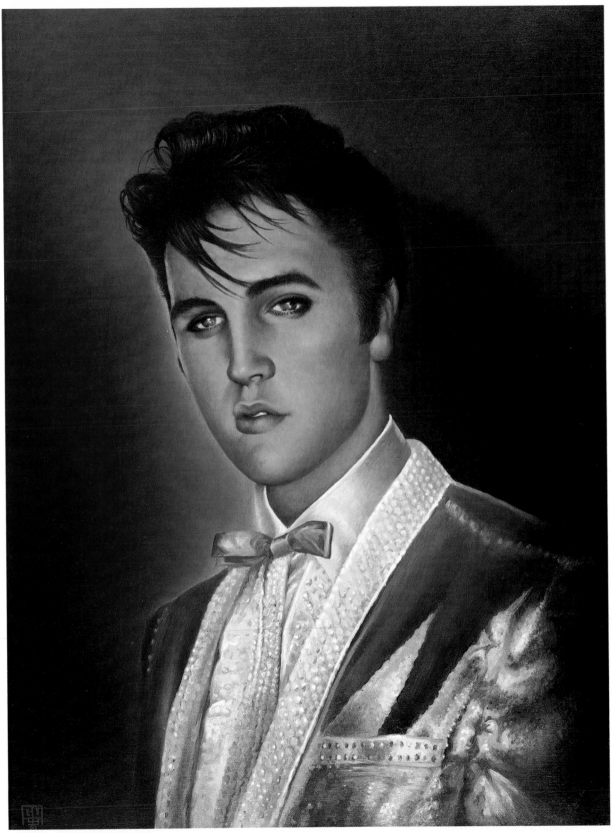

George Underwood

Acknowledgements

The author would like to thank Peter J. Taylor for his help, support and guidance throughout this project and for being a constant source of inspiration.

Very special thanks to:

Rhona F. Levene   Gary Withers   Stephanie Lipton   Emma Taylor   Jack Taylor
Susan Barnet   Linda Barnet   Geoff Green   Gordon Taylor   Mara Mira   Mize   David Reeson
Ken Rogers   Garey Gadson   Peter Stegmeyer   Laverte McDonald   Andrew Francis
Steve Coote   Judy Lipsey   Roger Semon   Just Janice   Billy Boy Rocka   Ger Rijff
Murry Keith of Memphis Magazine   Val Boyd   Miki Slingsby   Malgosia Van der Westelaken
Angelica Menheim   Dennis Berry   Chris Meiklejohn   Ian MacMeeking   Monte Dolack
Elisabeth A. Snyder   Christine Green   Marcia Terrones   Dinsdale Broderick   Caroline Taggart
Alison Craig   Brad Benedict   Fame 1 Crown/Harmony Publishers, New York
Fame 2 Indigo Books, New York

And to all the artists for their contributions and enthusiastic co-operation with this project

FOREWORD

Hey, hey, rock'n'roll! The music has never died, and the legend of Elvis Presley lives on. The truth of his life may be unravelling in some less than expected directions, to the fascination of many and the dismay of the devoted, but whatever the biographers may reveal the transcendent image is established. It is that of a young, dynamic and sensual man gyrating on a thousand American concert stages, exciting his enthralled and often hysterical fans to uncontrollable ardour, shaking the airwaves with the grinding rhythms of rock'n'roll. He was the acclaimed idol of an expressive and increasingly self-assertive youth culture.

For many of those special people who find themselves thrust before the eyes of the world, however, the gap between the image and the reality can be wide. In the case of Elvis, recent revelations suggest that it was cavernous. An unhappy and unattractive background behind the public glamour only seems to underline the enlarging and distorting power of the media. Girls dreamed of being alone with him, if only for a few moments; millions of boys wished to be like him, but the closest they came was in copying his hairstyle ('a vaseline cathedral', as *Life* magazine described it). Yet the Elvis who electrified the youth of nations staggered between personal crises, was often aggressive and indifferent to others, lost control of his own career while those around him prospered, and finally drifted into a destructive underlife of drug abuse. There is much to regret in the story of the whole man. In its later stages, the outward image becomes that of the established and rather safer super-star, veteran of an endless stream of escapist movies, a balladeer who played Las Vegas. On the road from sweaty dance-halls to the well-heeled showbar, he had become both hero and casualty of a musical revolution.

For rock'n'roll was not just a revelation – a movement that would radically change the direction of popular music – it *was* a benign revolution. Those with narrower minds saw it as degenerate and animalistic; others saw it as a vibrant triumph over the humdrum. And just as every movement has its creed, its uniforms, its propaganda, and its art, so too it was inevitable that Elvis, like the leaders of political and religious movements, would be captured before long on canvas and paper. Billboards, magazine covers, movie posters, greetings cards, record sleeves, and the fine art of the galleries – the images have swelled forth and multiplied a thousandfold.

The paintings and drawings in this book, gathered together for the first time, come from a remarkably wide range of sources, by artists in many countries. Their co-operation in reproducing them here is greatly appreciated. There are few generalisations to be made about the styles of artistic imagination represented in the collection; sometimes they are faithful to the photographic images, sometimes relying on caricature, sometimes romantic, and mostly shunning abstraction. We can let the pictures speak for themselves, however. In whatever manner the world's artists may have interpreted his presence, Elvis Presley helped to change a generation, and in so doing became a legend. It seems beyond doubt that his legend will endure. The life was only a beginning.

'Even today he don't seem growed up to me. I still see that little tow-head riding the trike we gave him when he was three round and round the kitchen.
Lots of parents don't let their children know when things are troubling them. I don't believe in that. Elvis would hear us worrying about our debts, being out of work and sickness and so on. He would say, "Don't you worry none, when I grow up, I'm going to buy you a fine house and pay everything you owe at the grocery store and get two Cadillacs – one for you and Daddy and one for me." Little as he was, the way he'd look up at me, holding onto my skirt – you know, I'd believe him.' '

Gladys Presley

'We figured if we went to Memphis there would be more money and it would be more fun for Elvis, but in the early days we were bitterly disappointed. His mother and I walked the streets looking for work. We did this even in heavy rain or snow but for quite a time, there was no work to be found. My wife and I tried to keep our troubles from Elvis, but he was sensitive and I'm sure he knew what was happening, even if we didn't talk about our problems out loud.'

Vernon Presley

Gunter Blum

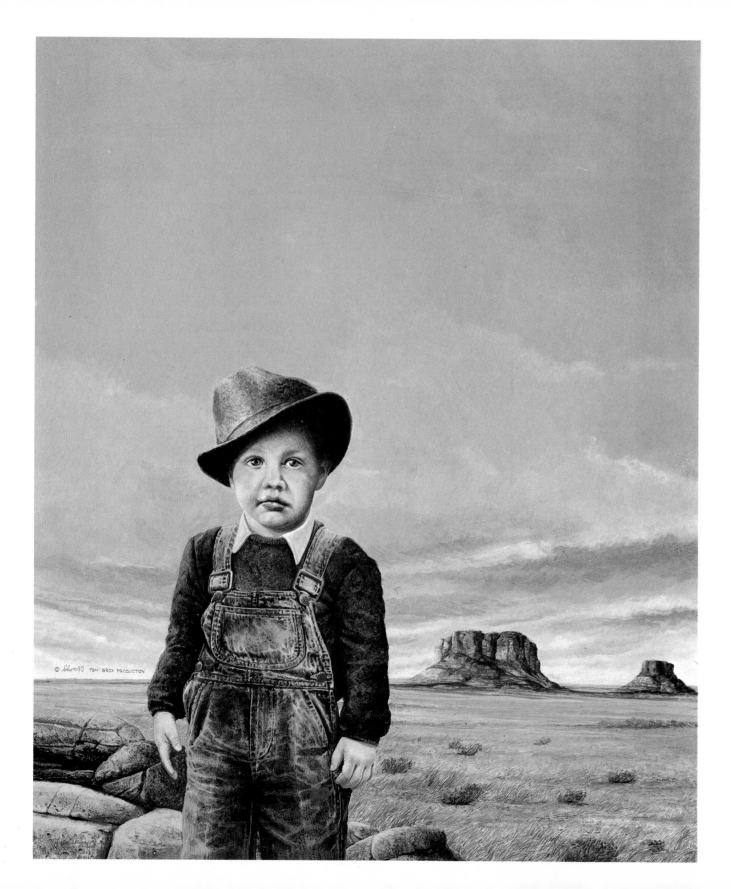

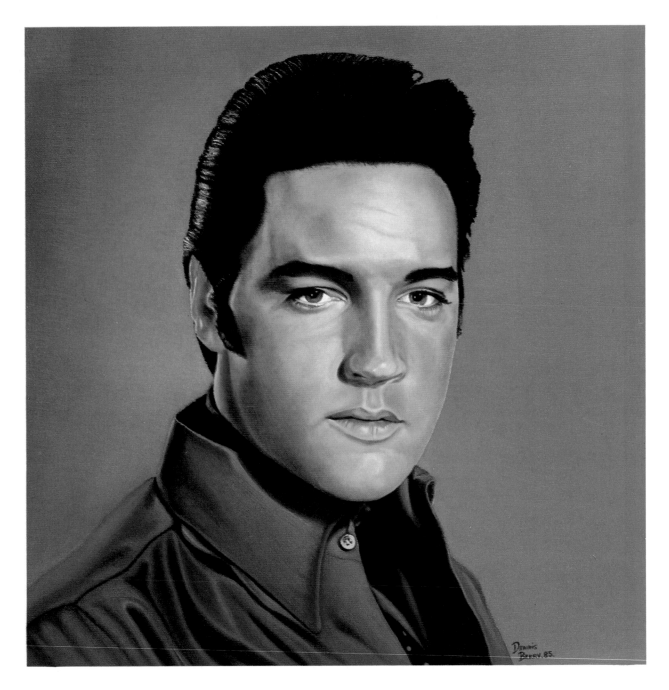

'He's naturally kind and thoughtful and good. Best of all, in spite of his huge success – he's unassuming.'

Connie Stevens

Dennis Berry

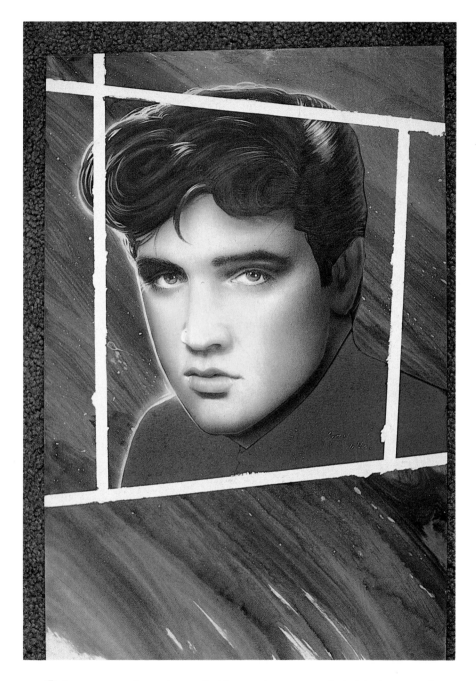

'Elvis was very down-to-earth. He made me comfortable, he wasn't aggressive with me and he never pushed. He was very gentle.'

Priscilla Presley

'Every morning when I woke up and looked out the window, there were at least two hundred kids lined up on the sidewalk outside, staring at the house. Some of them would stay there all day long, just trying to get a glimpse of him. And when he would go out, he was very sweet to them. A lot of people I know would get angry, or impatient – but Elvis is very sweet to the kids, very nice to them. He always spends as much time with them as he can, even though it tires him out.'

Natalie Wood

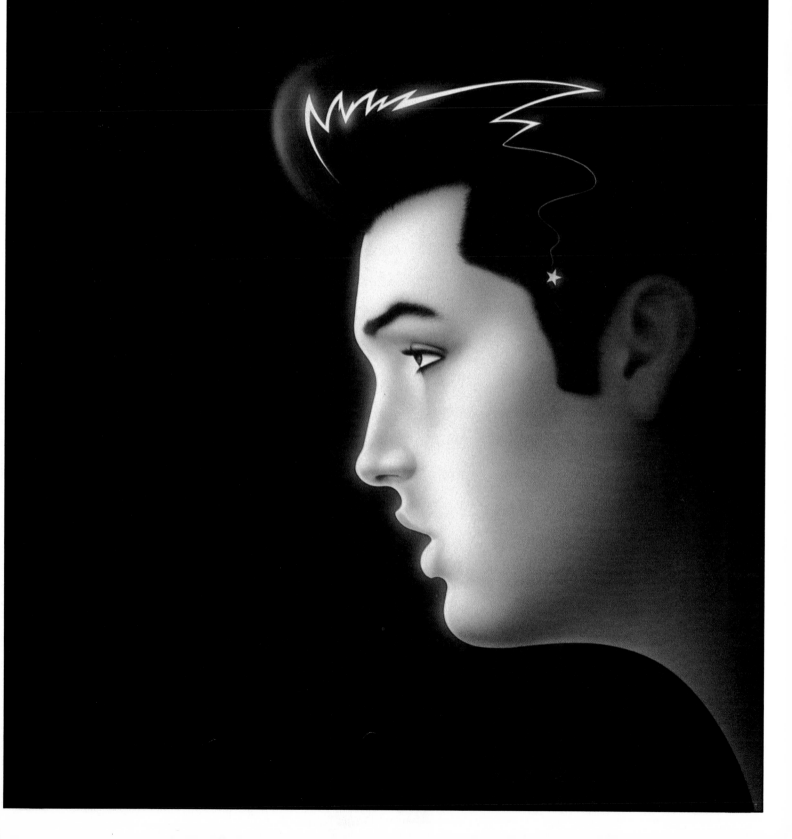

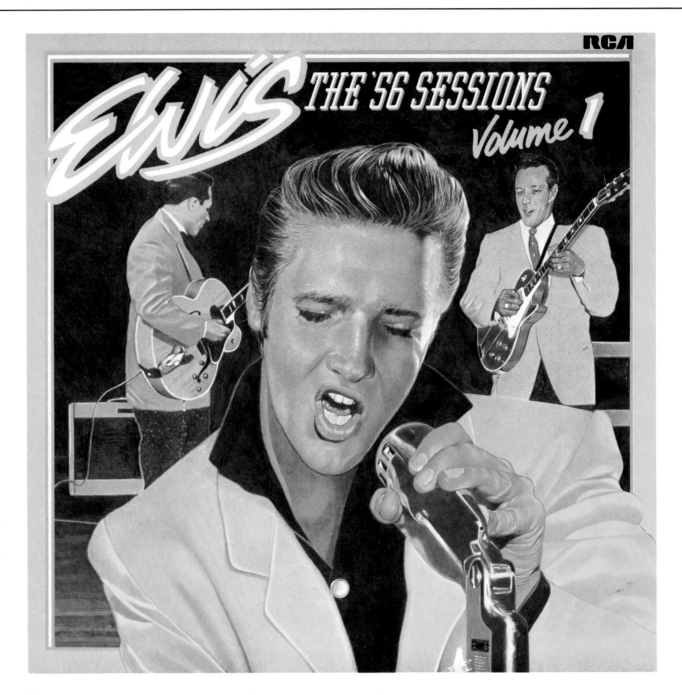

'I remember how he sat opposite me in his dressing room after one show —
his eyes aglow, his hair wild and straggly and his body running with sweat.
"Gee," he said, "It's great, wonderful, fantastic — being in the centre of all
that noise and excitement." Then he looked thoughtful and added, "I
wonder where it's all going to end."'

Johnny Tillotson

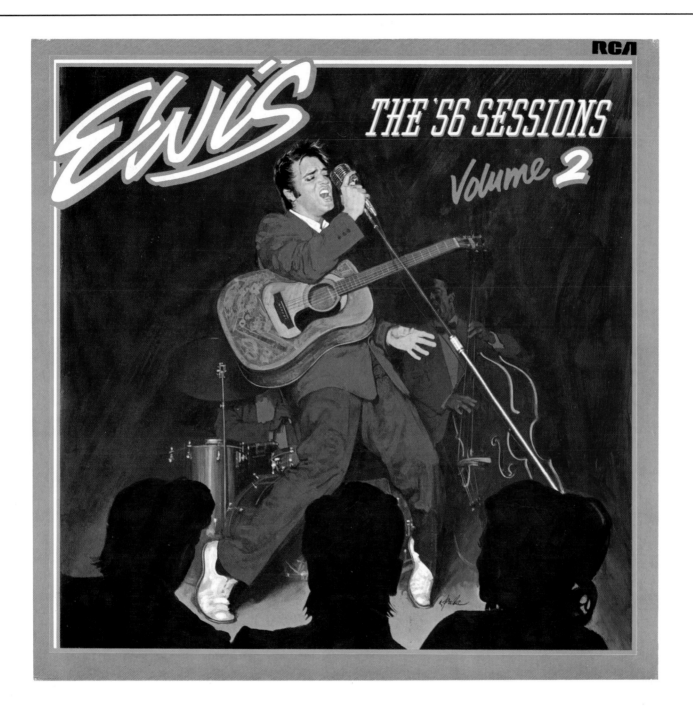

'Popular music has been sinking in this country for some years. Now it has reached its lowest depths in the "grunt and groin" antics of one Elvis Presley.'

Ben Gross

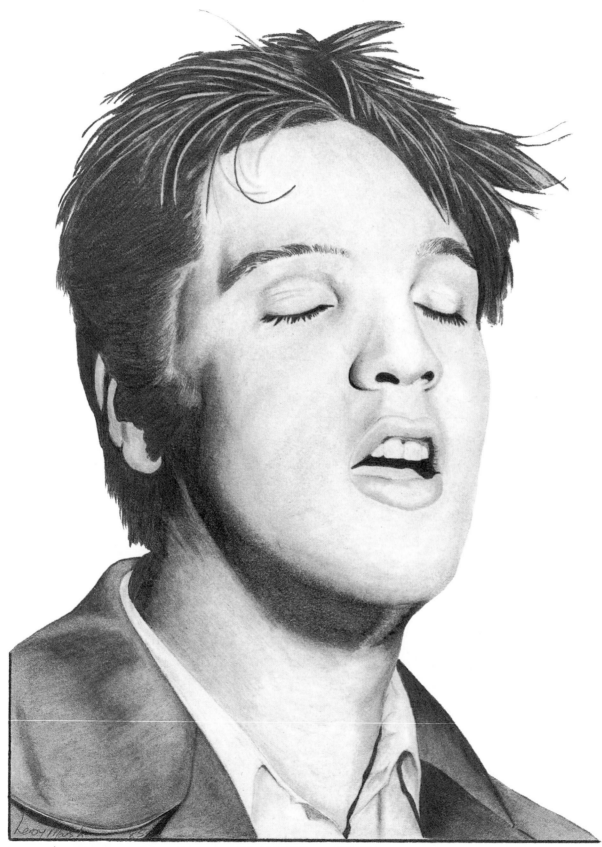

Leroy Marsh © Face of Art Designs

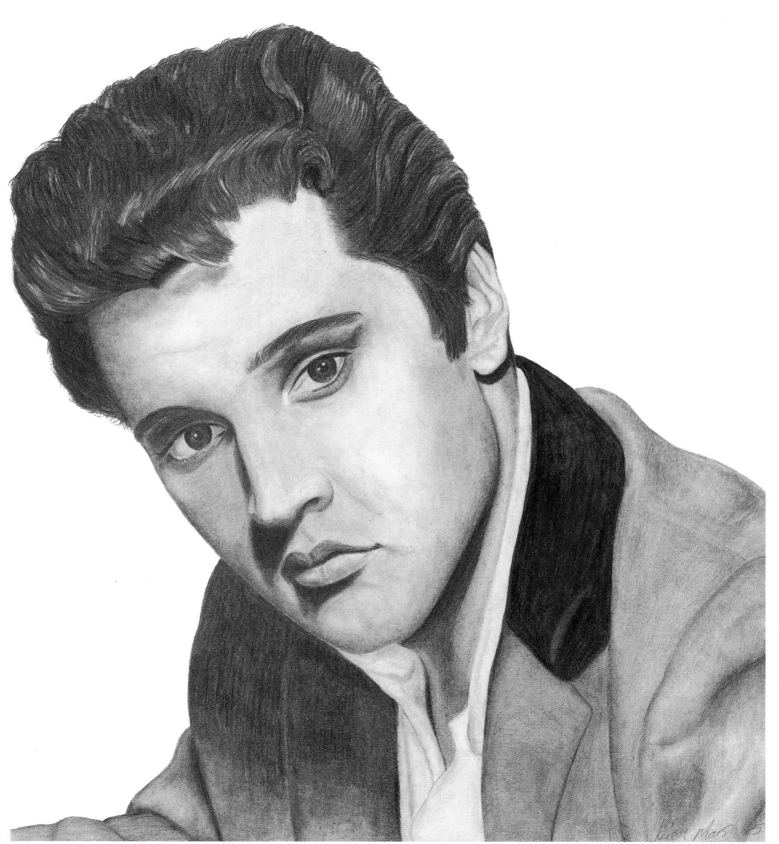

Leroy Marsh © Face of Art Designs

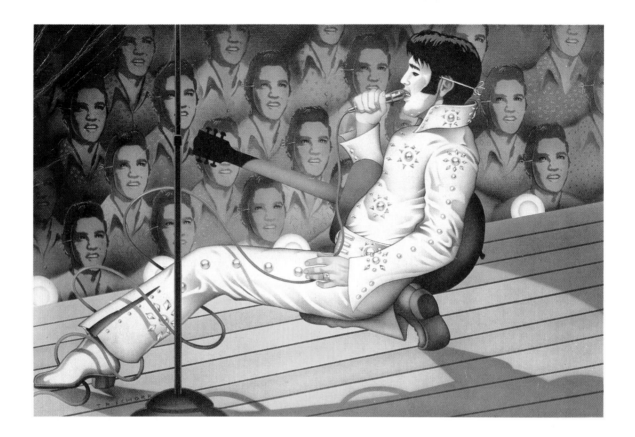

'It was just incredible in Vegas. I was kidding him. He introduced me and said, "Campbell, I understand you're doing an imitation of me. I just want you to know it will always be an imitation." And I said, "I'm not going to do it no more, I got to gain some weight first." He laughed and the audience went, "Ooh, hey, boo." I said, "Can't you take a joke?" And Elvis said, "Well, when you're down here next, I'm coming down and I'm gonna sit in the front row and read the newspaper and heckle." The audience laughed and I said, "Elvis, if I'm singing as good as you are, I won't care." '

Glen Campbell

'If Presley copied me, I don't care. More power to him. I'm not starving '

Bo Diddley

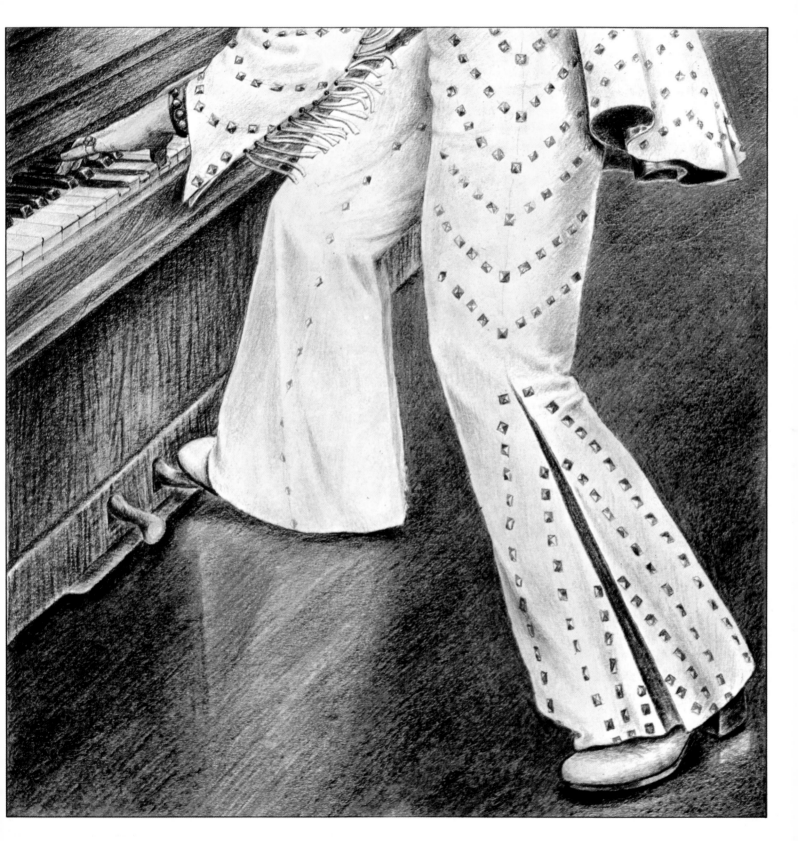

Valerie Hill

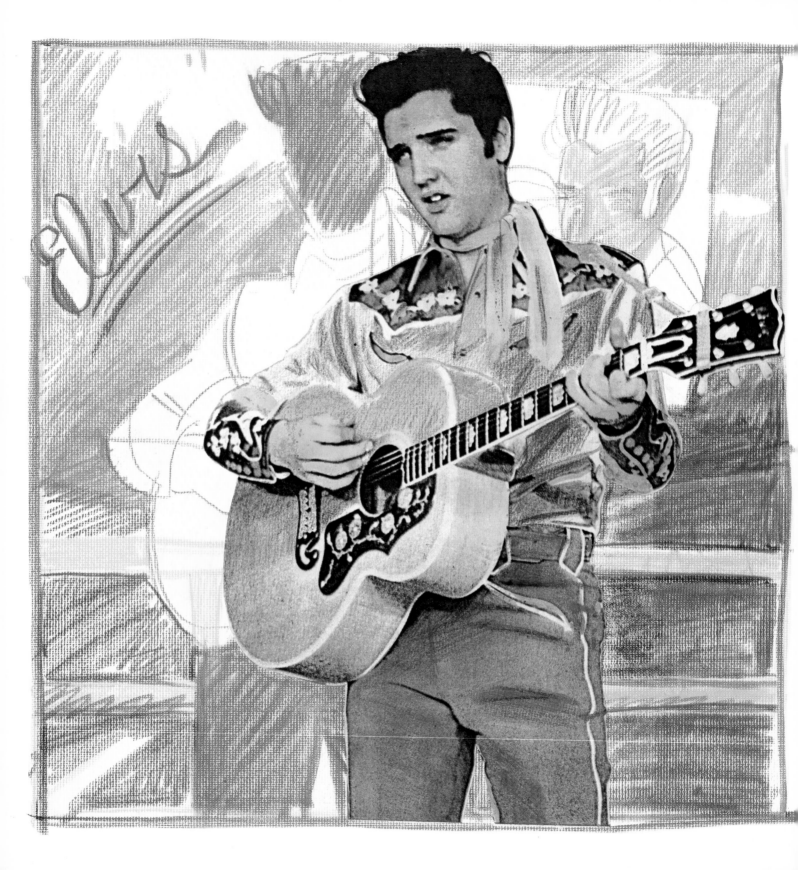

'Elvis was in a country music package when I first met him and the show came to my home town – Jacksonville, Florida – where I was a disc jockey. This must have been right at the start of Presley's career because he had gone out with the package as first act on, but that arrangement hadn't lasted long because he had whipped up such riotous behaviour among fans the show had almost been brought to a halt. So they had switched him to last act.'

Johnny Tillotson

'There was something just bordering on rudeness about Elvis. He never actually did anything rude, but he always seemed as if he was just going to. On a scale of one to ten, I would rate him eleven.'

Sammy Davis Jnr

'People say I'm vulgar. They say I use my hips disgustingly. But that's my way of putting over a song. I have to move. When I have a lot of energy, I move more. I lose three or four pounds a performance. I've always done it this way.'

Elvis Presley

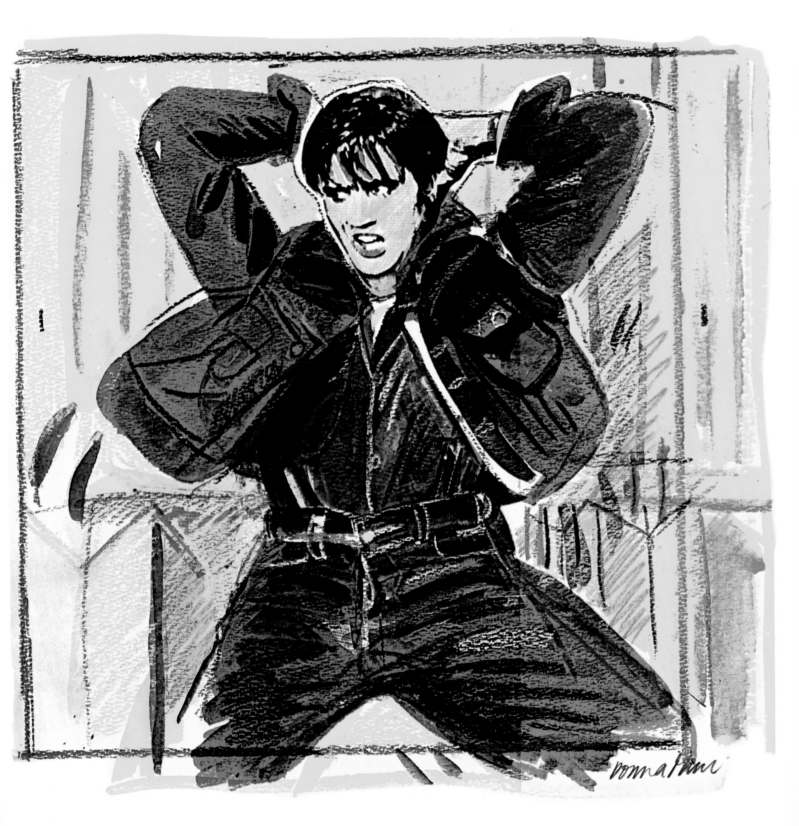

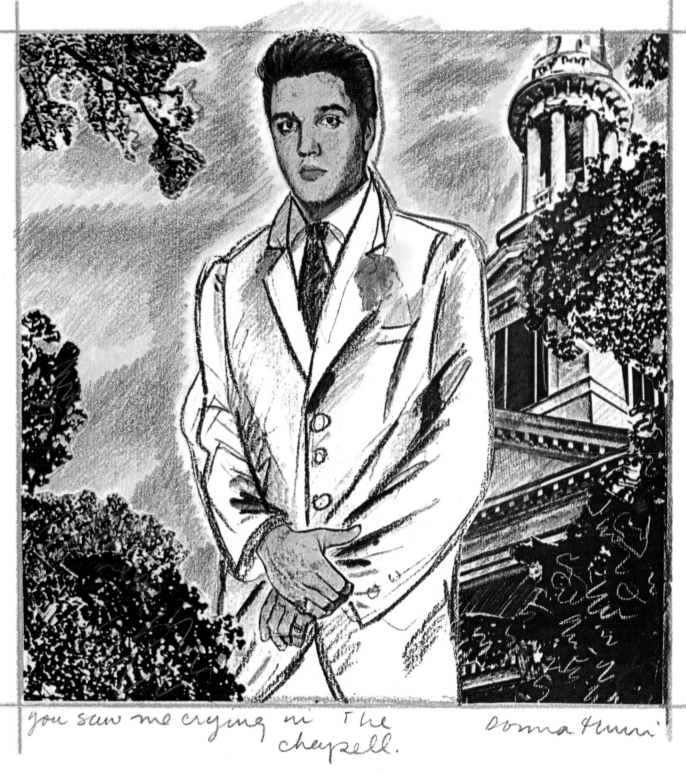

you saw me crying in the chappell.

Donna Muir

'From what I've heard I'm not sure I'd want my children to see him.'

Billy Graham

Donna Muir

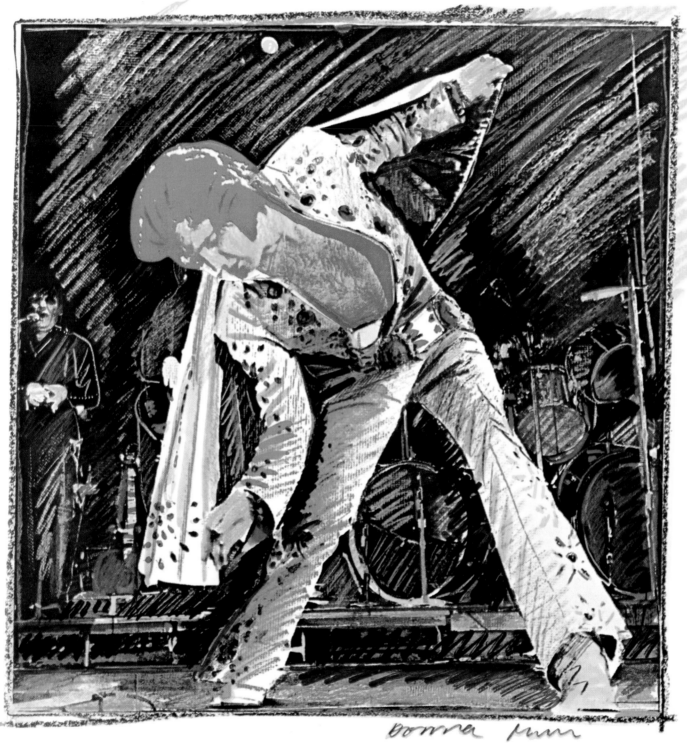

'At 9.15, Elvis appeared, materialized, in a white suit of lights, shining with golden appliqués, the shirt front slashed to show his chest. Around his shoulders was a cape lined in a cloth of gold, it's collar faced with scarlet. It was anything you wanted to call it, gaudy, vulgar, magnificent.'

New York Times

Donna Muir

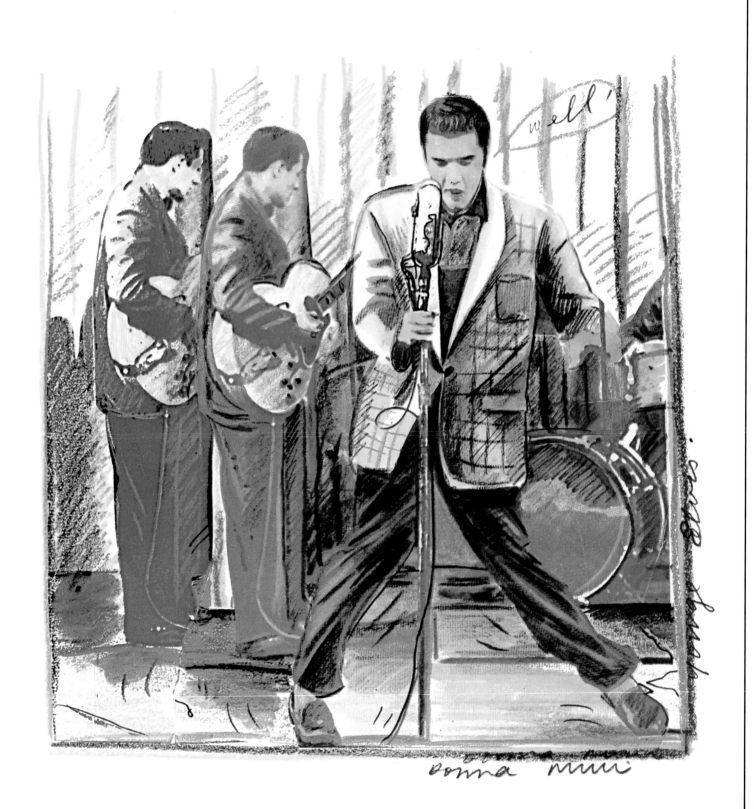

Donna Muir

'In Kansas City one night, I started to sing . . . and six thousand of them ran for the stage. Ah ran through a door, but they took the door right off the hinges as they came after me. Ah ran back into the alley wheah the car was waitin' . . . Theah was this one right on my heels, and when Ah slammed the door of the car, she kept right on comin'. Ran her nose right into the door.'

Elvis Presley

'I knew he'd be a hit. Anybody who could make that much noise has gotta be a hit. But I was sure he couldn't last, and I still am. Johnnie Ray – now, there's an entertainer. He's got some class. Presley's got nothing but bumps and grinds.'

Jackie Gleason

'You Memphis politicians had better watch out if Elvis Presley ever decides
to enter politics.'

George Bush

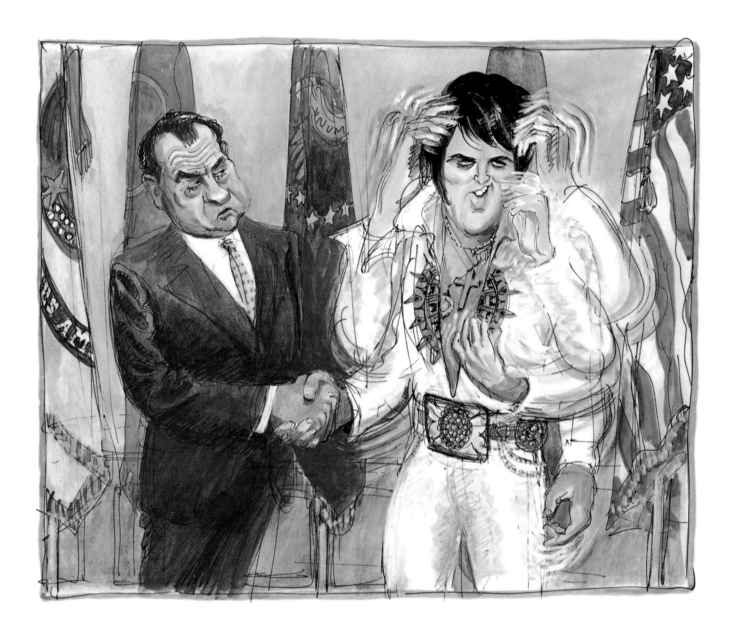

Edward Sorel

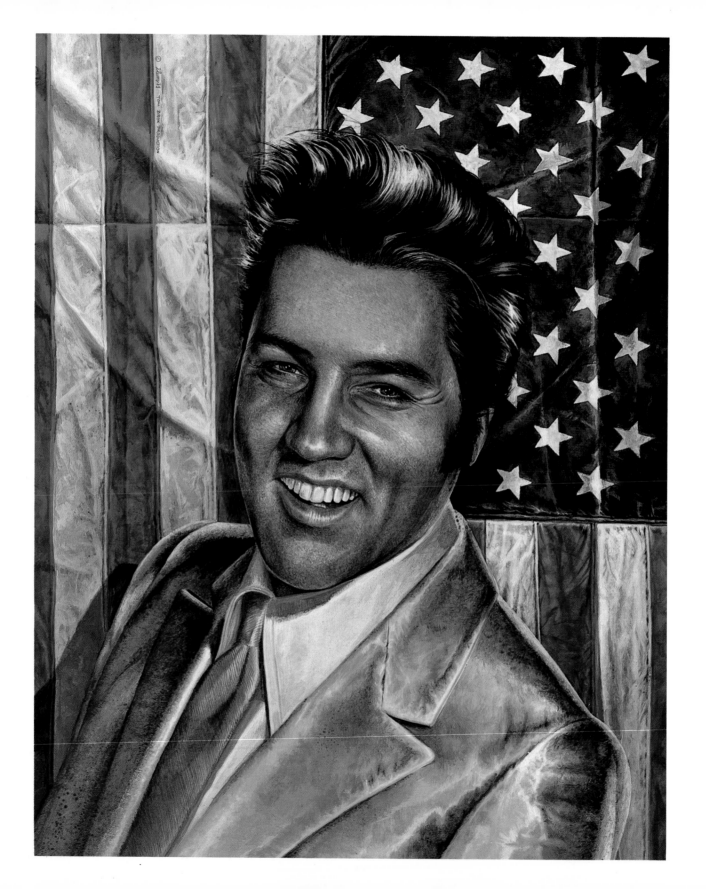

'Elvis Presley's death deprives our country of a part of itself. His music and his personality, fusing the styles of white country and black rhythm and blues, permanently changed the face of American popular culture. His following was immense and he was a symbol to the people the world over of the vitality, rebelliousness and good humour of this country. He burst upon the scene more than twenty years ago with an impact that was unprecedented and will probably never be equalled.'

Jimmy Carter

'He was as big as the whole country itself, as big as the whole dream. He just embodied the essence of it and he was in mortal combat with the thing. Nothing will ever take the place of that guy.'

Bruce Springsteen

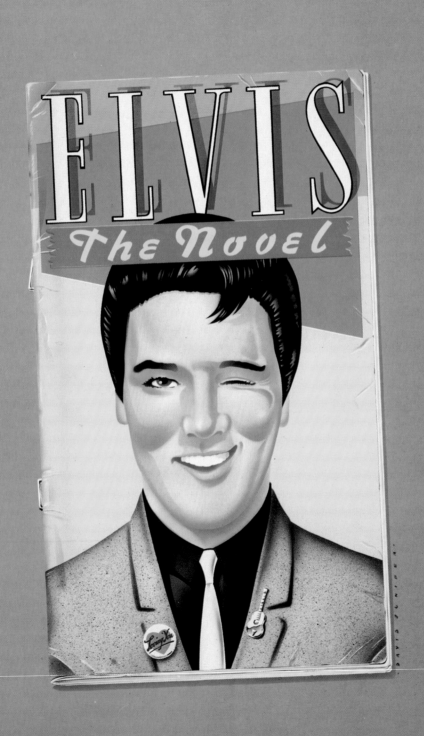

'He can do anything. He would be a dream to direct. His comedy timing is faultless.'

George Cukor

David Juniper

'It was quite extraordinary. Elvis walked onto the set to do his test with a veteran actor named Frank Faylen. I hadn't a clue how he would cope but after a few minutes I knew he was a natural. Like Sinatra and with just as much personality. He's going to be one of the biggest stars ever to come out of this place.'

Hal Wallis

'People say Elvis's pictures aren't doing so good these days. I tell you, we've made twenty-two pictures, nineteen have been box office successes, two haven't completed their run yet and the other one hasn't been released. How do you argue with this kind of success? It's like telling Maxwell House to change their coffee formula when the stuff is selling like no tomorrow.'

Colonel Tom Parker

'It's incredible! Presley has caused more fuss out here than Marilyn Monroe. Girls hang around in crowds and every day, more and more sackloads of Presley fan mail are arriving and long-distance calls from all over the world are flooding our switchboards.'

Studio official

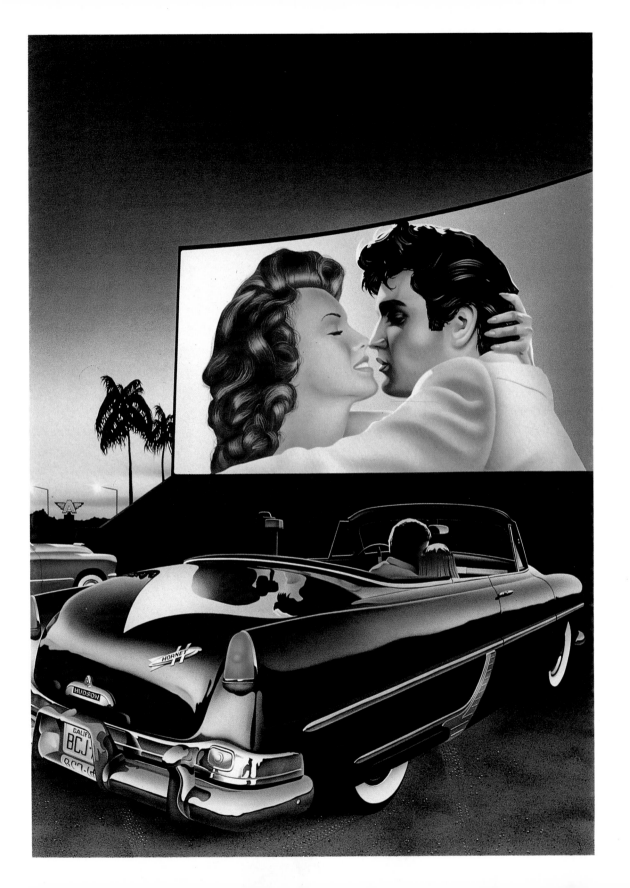

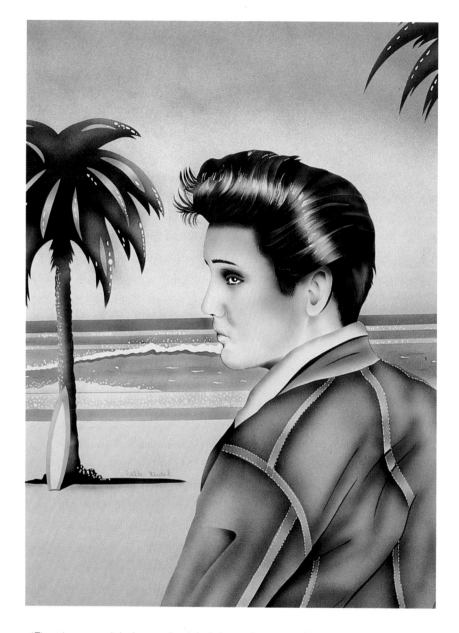

'That boy could charm the birds from the trees. He was so eager and
humble, we went out of our way to help him.'

Richard Egan

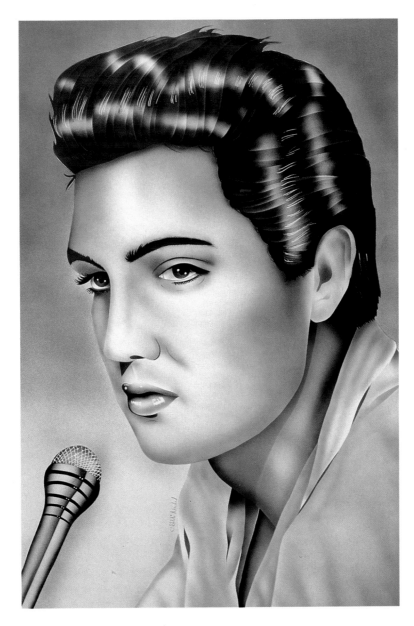

'He's a very well-mannered and sensitive person – just like me.'

Ursula Andress

Clothilde Nadel

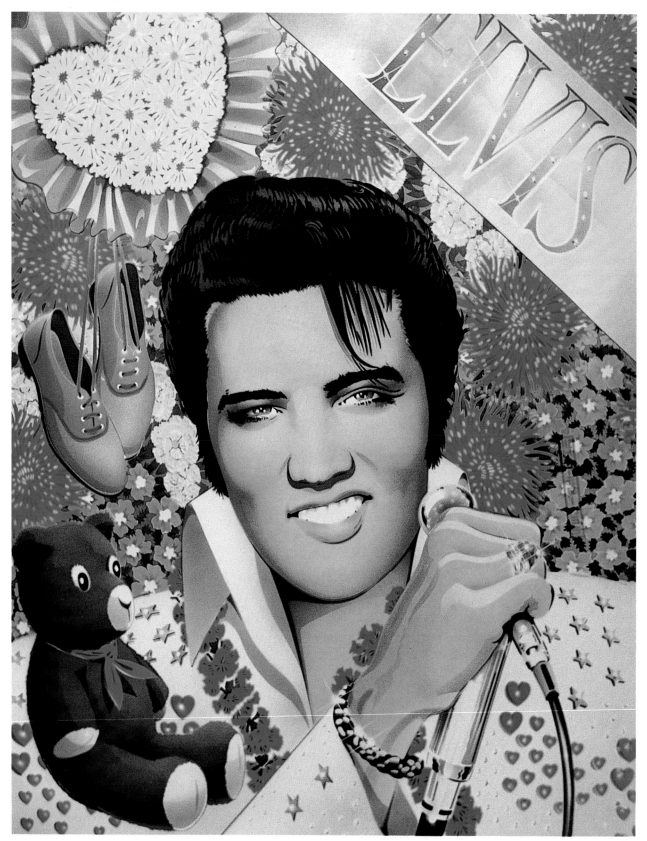

Kim Whitesides

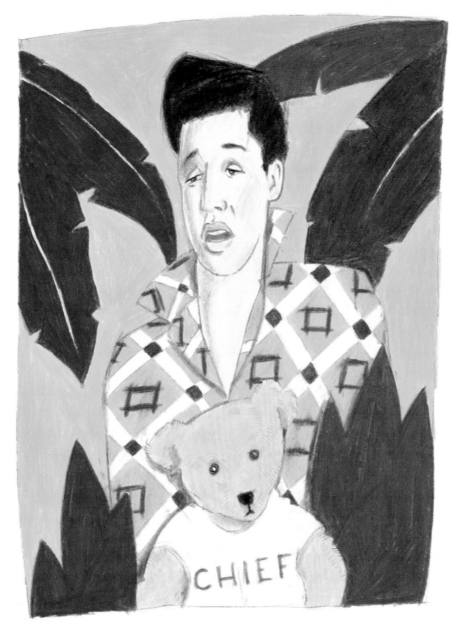

'I've never seen anything like the madness that surrounds Presley. He could never go anywhere without causing a sensation. That's still why he doesn't want to be seen anywhere, he's basically a very ordinary, very nice man who can't see why he should be singled out in this way.'

Natalie Wood

David Reeson

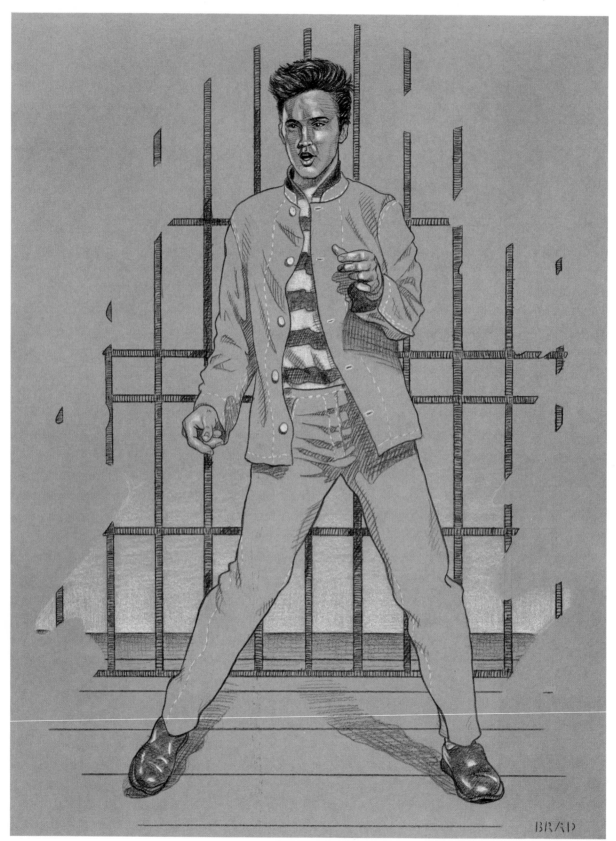

Brad Marshall

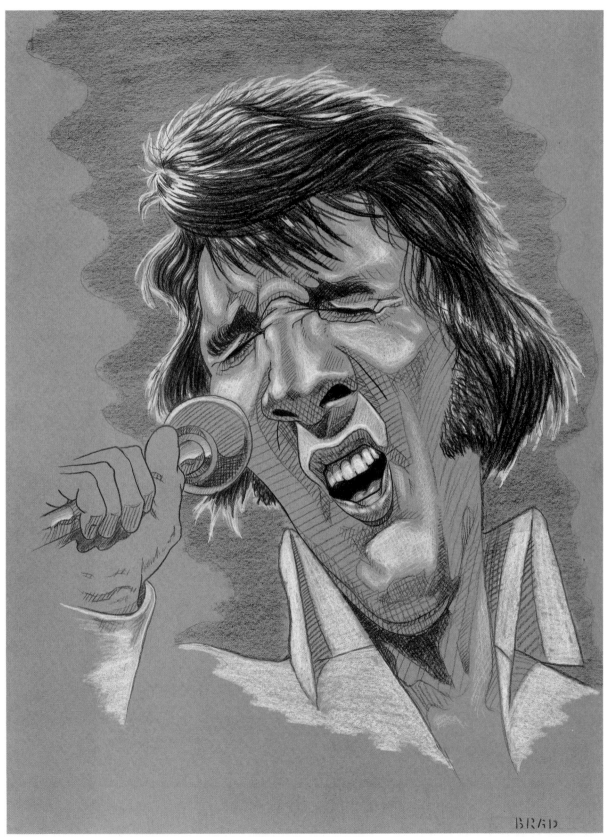

Brad Marshall

'Elvis was the King of Rock and Roll because he was the embodiment of its sins and virtues, grand and vulgar, rude and elegant, powerful and frustrated, absurdly simple and awesomely complex. He was the King, I mean, in our hearts, which is the place where the music really comes to life. And just as Rock and Roll will stand as long as our hearts beat, he will always be our king; forever, irreplaceable, corrupt and incorruptible, beautiful and horrible, imprisoned and liberated – and, finally, rockin' and free, free at last.'

Dave Marsh

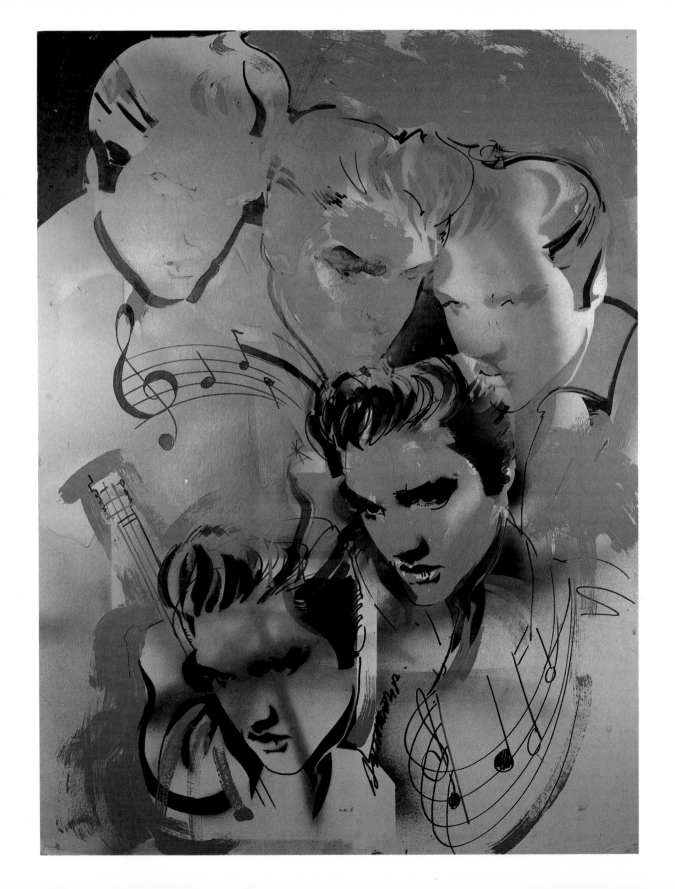

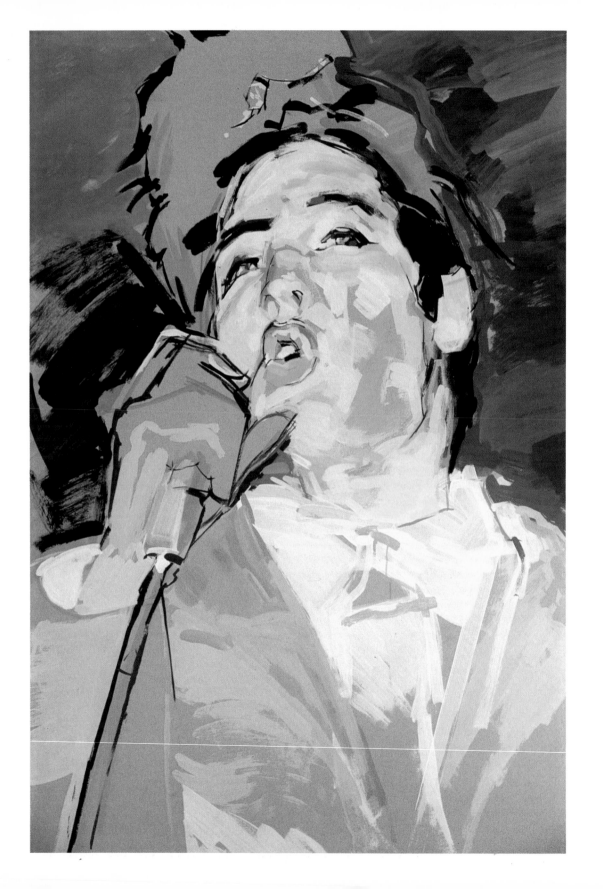

'Blacks didn't have the air-waves Elvis had. He delivered what he obtained beautifully.'

Chuck Berry

'He was an integrator. Elvis was a blessing. They wouldn't let Black music through. He opened the door for Black music.'

Little Richard

'He was white, but he sang Black. It wasn't socially acceptable for white kids to buy Black records at the time. Elvis filled a void.'

Chet Atkins

'Elvis is the greatest Blues singer in the world today.'

Joe Cocker

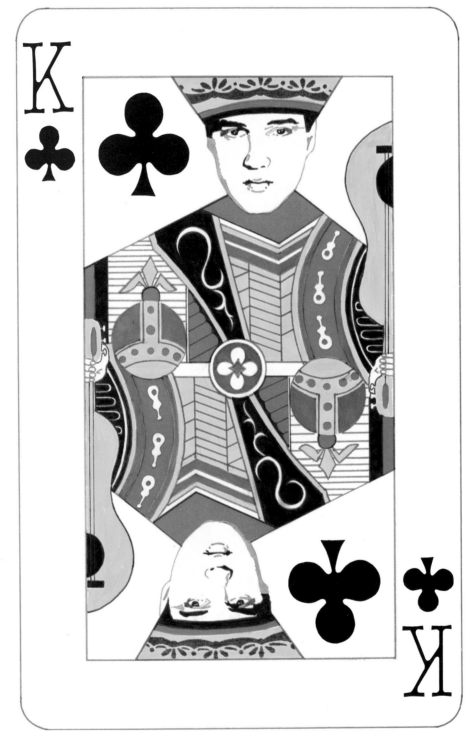

'There's no way to measure his impact on society or the void that he
leaves. He will always be the King of rock'n'roll.'

Pat Boone

Roger G. Taylor

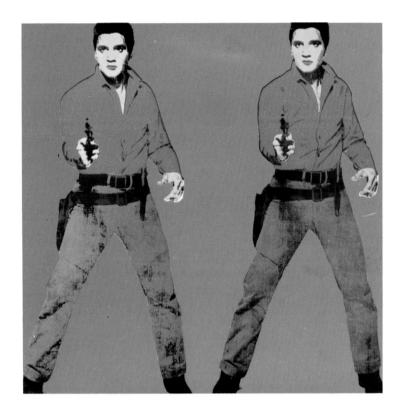

'If you looked closely at Elvis – as pop artist Andy Warhol did – you saw an almost androgynous softness and passivity in his punk-hood persona.'

Newsweek
29 August 1977

'He was not primitive, like people think. He was an artist, and he was into being an artist, of course, he was also into rocking his ass off, but that was part of it. Onstage he encompassed everything – he was laughing at the world and he was laughing at himself, but at the same time, he was dead serious . . .

Bruce Springsteen

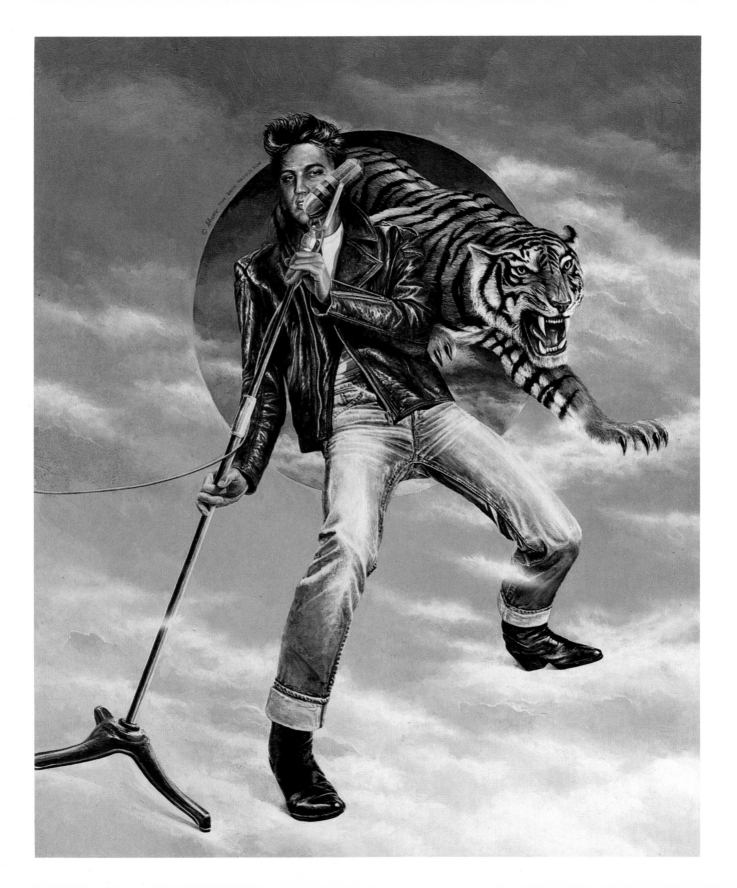

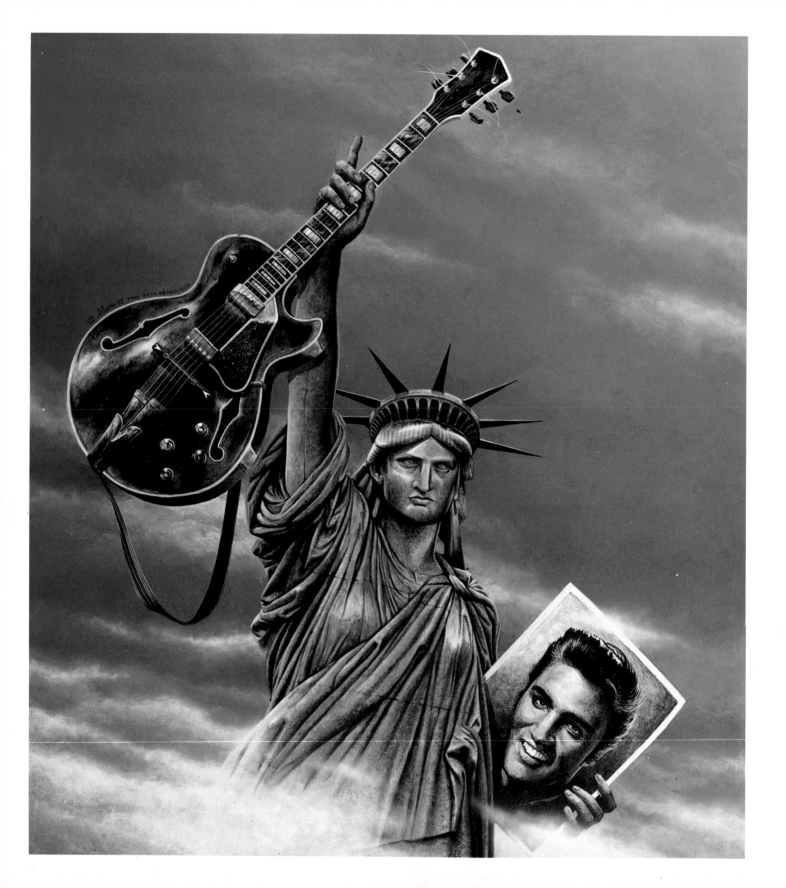

'Elvis Presley remains one of the quintessential American pop stars, gaudy, garish, compromised in his middle age in commercial consideration, yet gifted with an enormous talent and a charismatic appeal beyond mere nostalgia. Presley remains a true American artist – one of the greatest in American popular music, a singer of native brilliance and a performer of magnetic dimensions.'

Jim Millar
Rolling Stone

'He didn't drink, he didn't swear. He didn't even smoke. It was like having the date that I never ever had in high school. I thought it was really wild.'

Natalie Wood

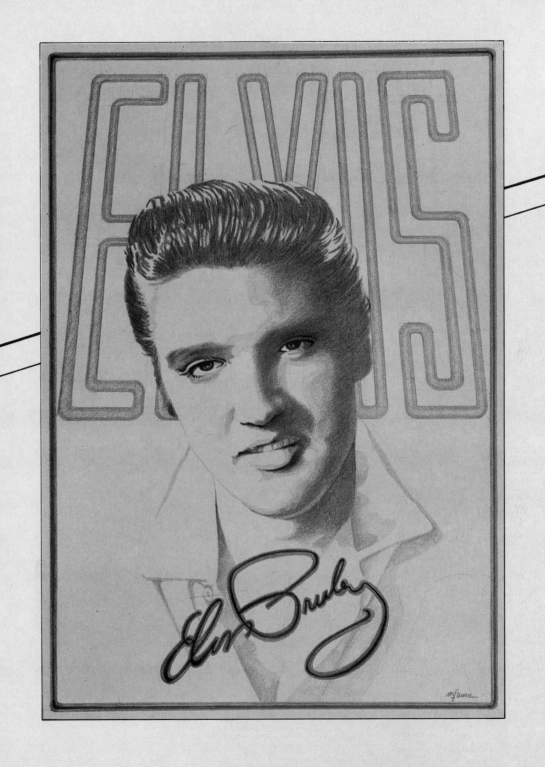

'I am not exactly one of the in-crowd but I've long had a deep respect for Elvis Presley. I don't regard his movies as being classics of the screen, but I regard his personality and sheer sense of style as being outstanding. To be honest, I don't collect pop records as such – I'd much rather play classical or show albums for personal relaxation. But I find his records stimulating and – well – fun! He has a deep voice that is instantly recognizable and that is obviously the secret of his staying power. I'd say he has more versatility too, than the rest of the pop singers. He sings a ballad with warmth but when he really lets himself go on a rock 'n' roll number . . . well, that is when he becomes truly exciting to hear. I doubt if I will ever work with Elvis Presley, but my admiration for his own kind of work is really boundless.'

Dirk Bogarde

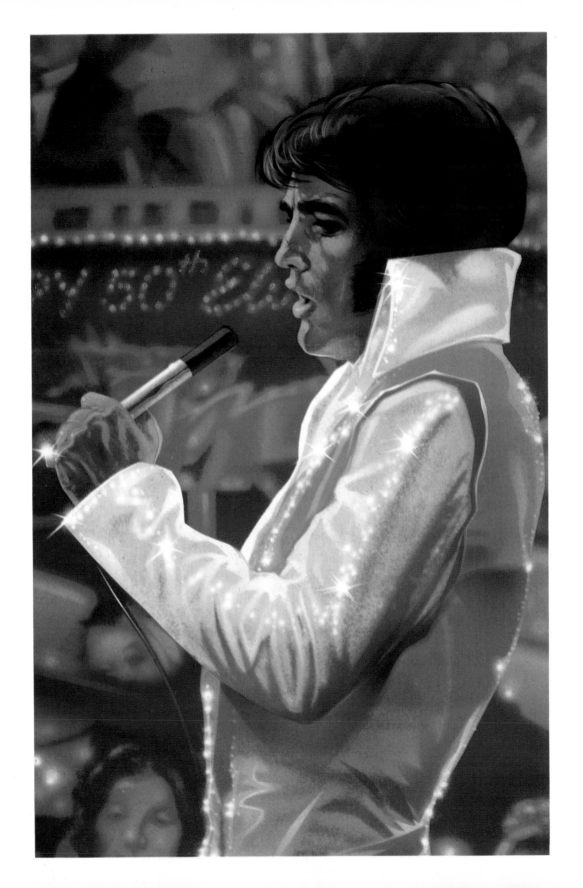

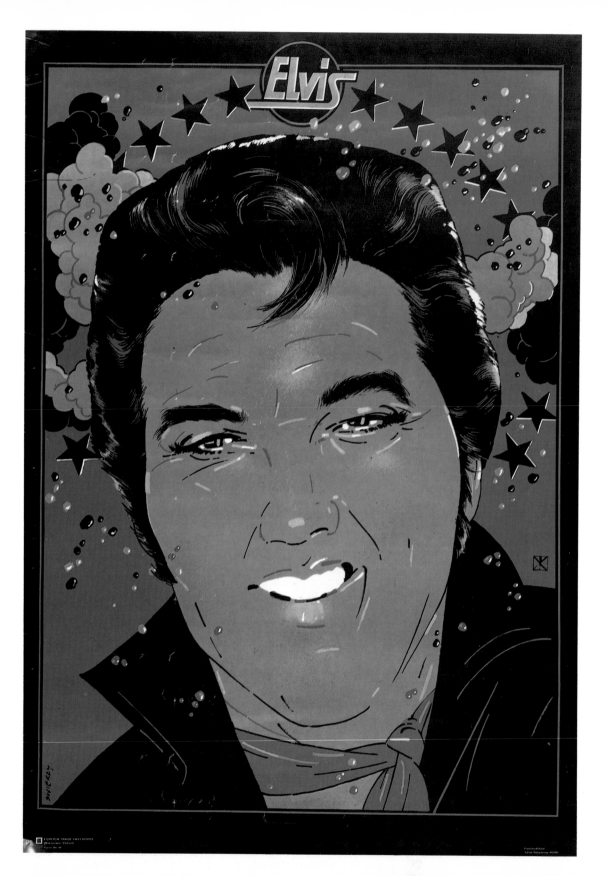

'For Elvis there was no escape in art, since his original triumph was his very artlessness. He didn't write songs, nor did he aspire to anything more than being successful. Even his films were no more than a magnification of his image, a further reinforcement of the impossible perfection which transformed him, like all our public figures, from a living presence into an all-purpose, economy-rate icon.'

Peter Gurnalnick
Country Music
December 1977

Waldemar Swierzy

'So Elvis Presley came, strumming a weird guitar and wagging his tail across the continent, ripping off fame and fortune as he scrunched his way, and, like a latter-day Johnny Appleseed, sowing seeds of a new rhythm and style in the white souls of the new white youth of America, whose inner hunger and need was no longer satisfied with the antiseptic white shoes and whiter songs of Pat Boone. ' "You can do anything," sang Elvis to Pat Boone's white shoes, "but don't you step on my Blue Suede Shoes!" '

Eldridge Cleaver
Soul On Ice

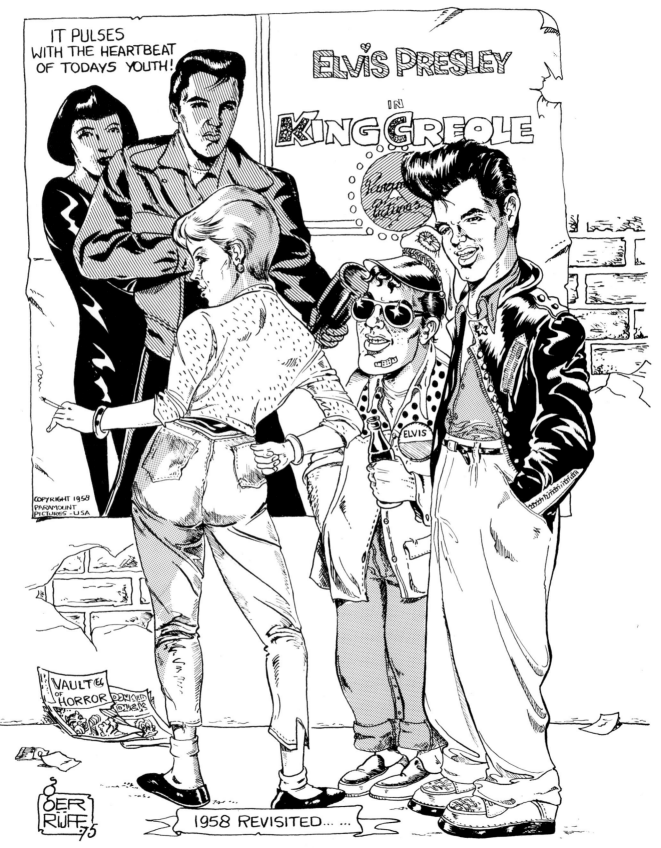

Ger Rijff

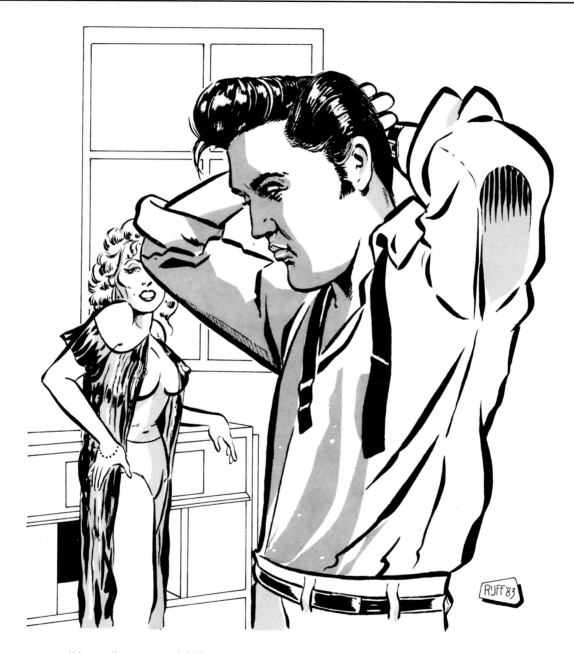

'He really wants to idolize womanhood, but there is a Victorian fascination with wicked women. He dislikes mature or older women, prefers the young girls and the mother images. He has very strong sex drives, but a lot of his sexual energy is sublimated in his work. Sex is important mainly as a physical need. He is also hung up on ritual and fetishes.'

Antonia Lamb
in *Elvis, a Biography*
Jerry Hopkins

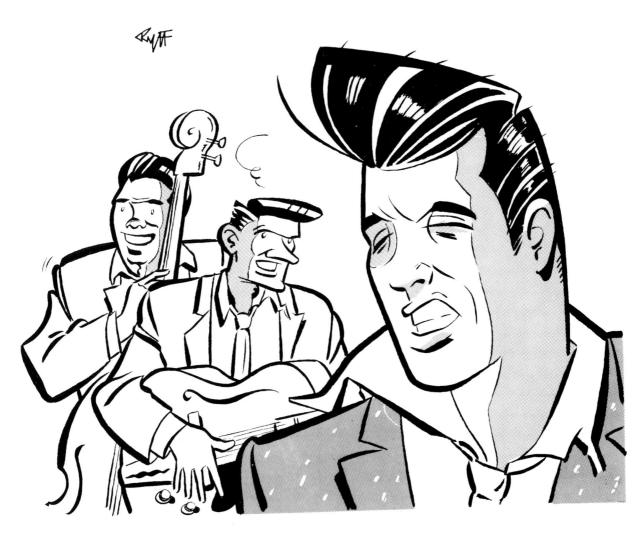

'I'd like to say to Elvis Presley and the country that this is a decent, fine boy and wherever you go, Elvis, and the guys who accompany you over there that we've never had a pleasanter experience in our show with a big name than we've had with you. You're thoroughly all right.'

Ed Sullivan

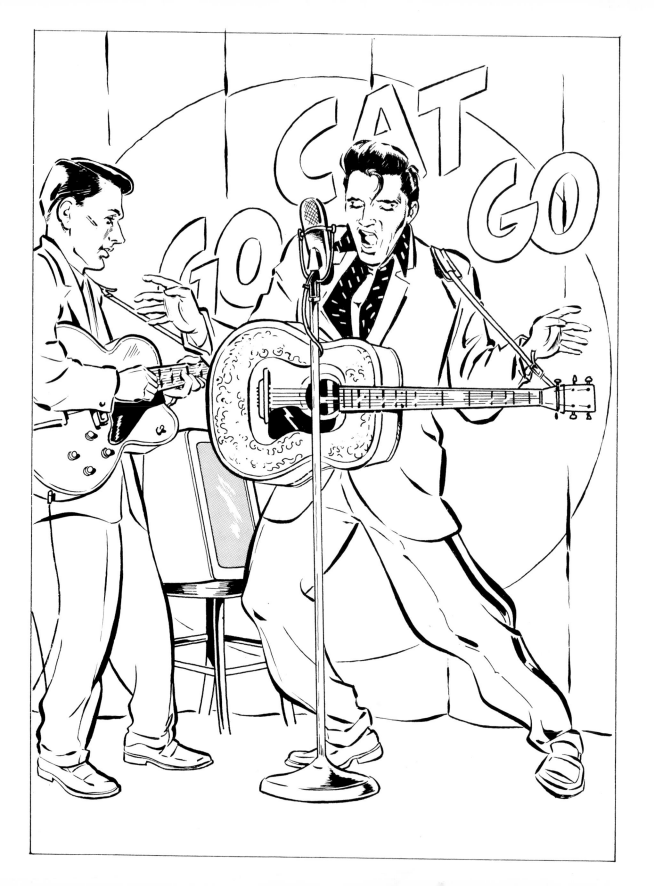

'The first time we met was at a record hop in Cleveland where Elvis was my supporting act, which was the only time that happened. I never again wanted to follow Elvis. I was very glad I had this big hit record going for me so that when I came on stage it wasn't totally anticlimatic.'

Pat Boone

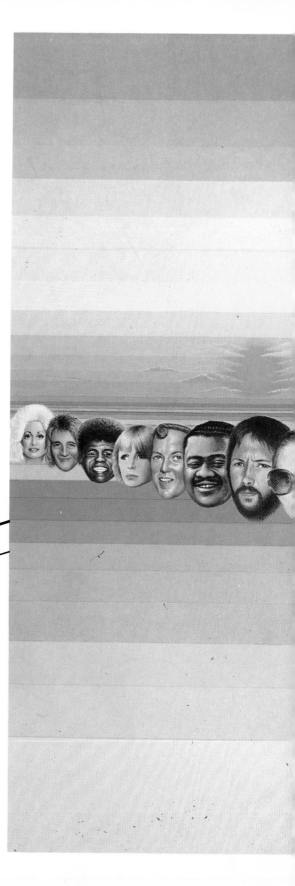

'Before there was Elvis, there was nothing.'

John Lennon

'People like myself, Mick Jagger and the others only really followed in his footsteps.'

Rod Stewart

'What he did was a part of history.'

Bing Crosby

'None of us could have made it without Elvis.'

Buddy Holly

George Underwood

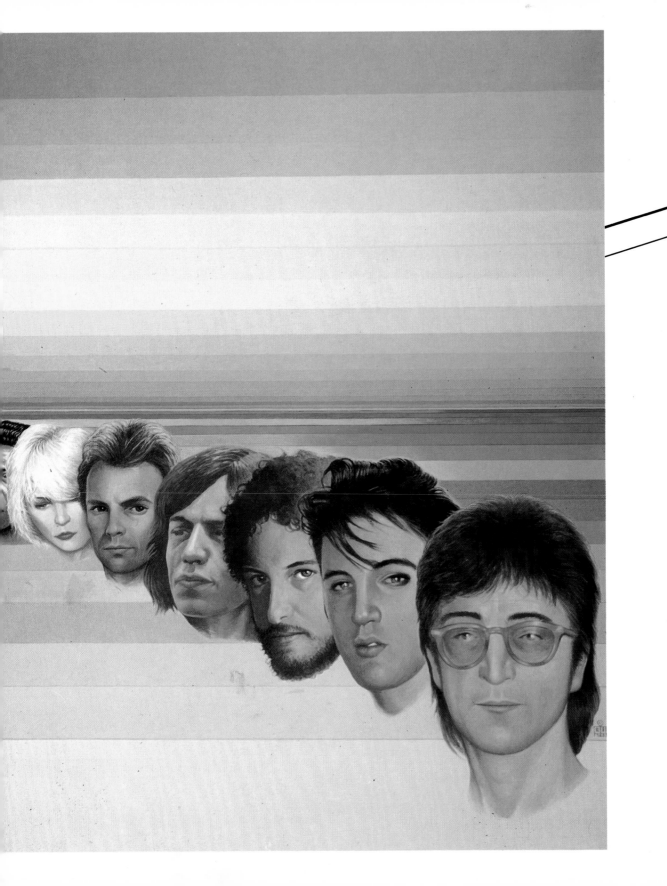

'Elvis Presley was a beautiful young person, right, whose recordings were just colossally great. But basically the best stuff he ever did was on the Sun record label. And then he got involved with Colonel Parker and went to RCA and then went the Hollywood way. The whole thing became completely ruined.'

Mark Knopfler

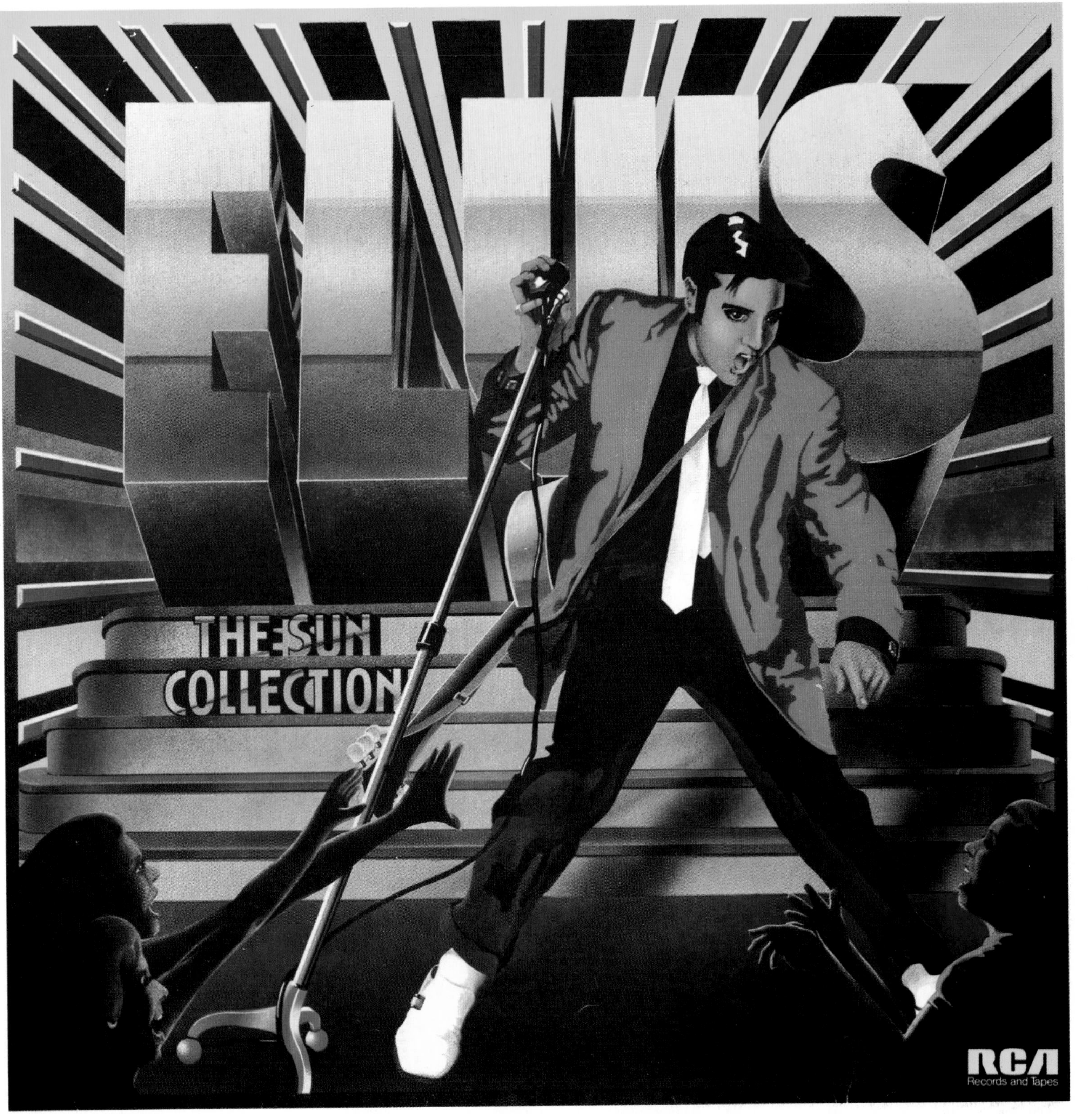
ELVIS
THE SUN
COLLECTION
RCA
Records and Tapes

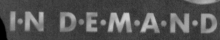

ELVIS

I·N D·E·M·A·N·D

'Elvis is outstanding. He has great talent, handles himself beautifully, hasn't followed the dope route, has kept his head on his shoulders and is to be admired. No wonder he's the top attraction in America. Presley is here to stay.'

Guy Lombardo

'There's got to be a valid reason why he's the most successful guy of the past decade. He's a giant, and any man who can influence all those people must have something. He's had expert guidance, of course, but there was a lot to guide.'

Isaac Hayes

'His body takes on a frantic quiver, as if he had swallowed a
jack-hammer.'

Time Magazine

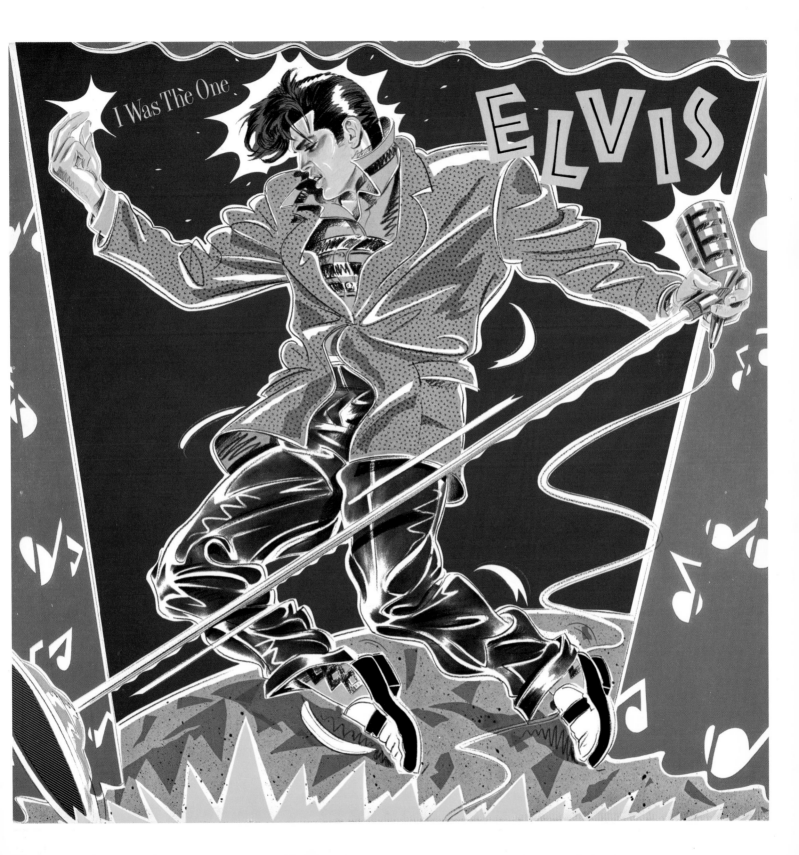

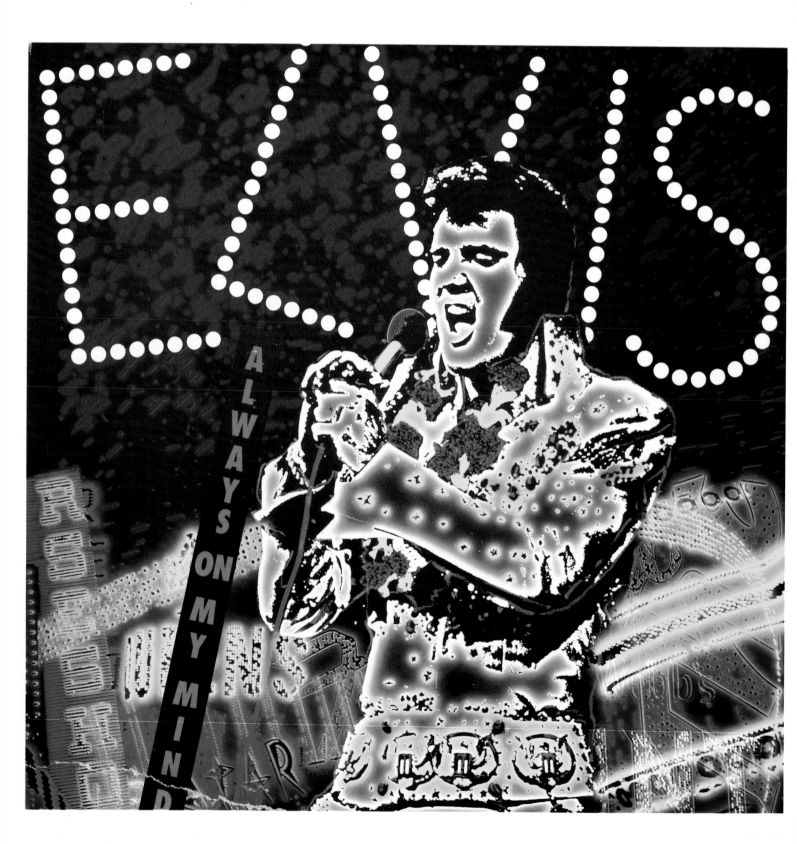

'Certain performers have an electric, magnetic quality – an ability to communicate a kind of excitement to an audience the minute they step up in front of one. Dietrich has it, Noel Coward has it, the late Fred Allen had it. And in some way I don't quite understand, this kid Presley has it, too.'

Steve Allen

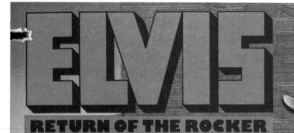

'I get chased all over the world, get my clothes ripped up, people screaming. But in my home, in Augusta, everything is cool. I wouldn't have it no other way, couldn't live if I couldn't walk the streets I grew up on. Now Elvis, he got so far away from it he couldn't do that. We were friends for a long time, for twenty years. And he told me, he'd ride around Memphis, around the streets he'd come up in, all alone at night. Ride around on his motorcycle when he was sure the rest of the world was asleep, just kind of hauntin' them places he hung around in as a kid. He was a country boy. But the way they had him living, they never turned off the air conditionin'. Took away all the good air. You get sick from that.'

James Brown

'Elvis Presley and rock'n'roll are making as much noise around the discussion table as on the turntable. For the past couple of months, The Beat and The Pelvis have been topics for educators, theologians, psychiatrists and assorted eggheads. Nothing much seems to have been solved, but it's been making for lively rhetoric.'

Variety
1956

Dennis Berry

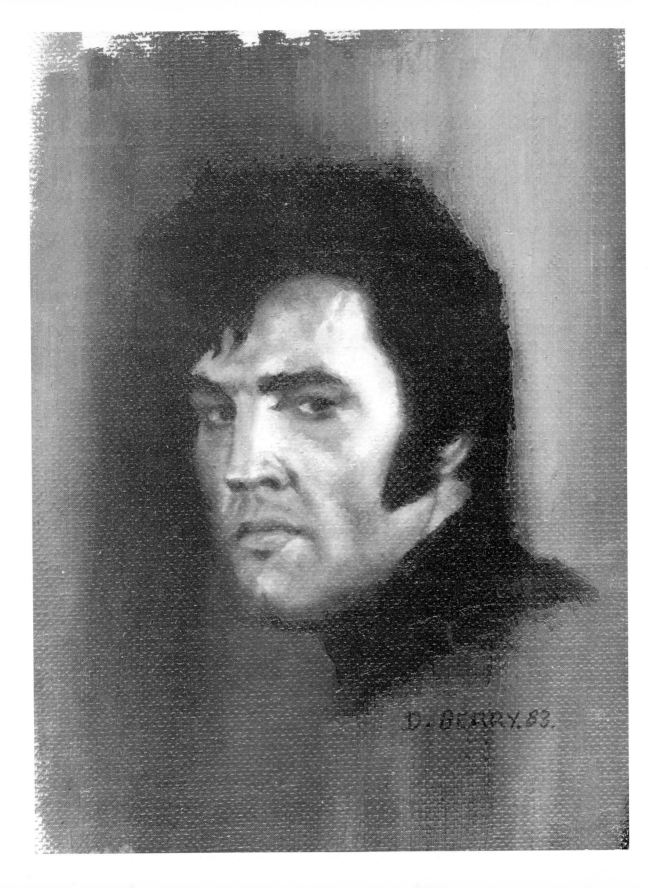

D. GERRY. 83.

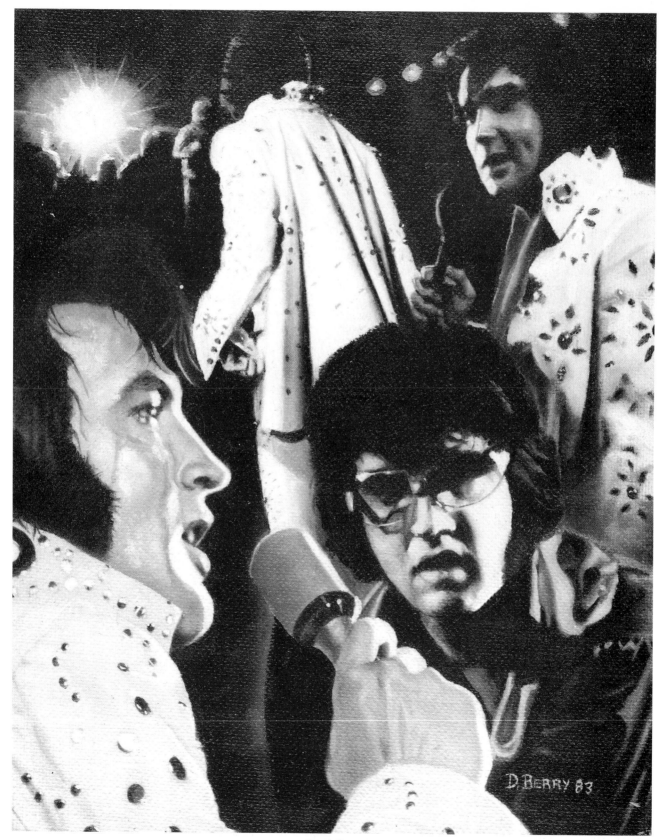

Dennis Berry

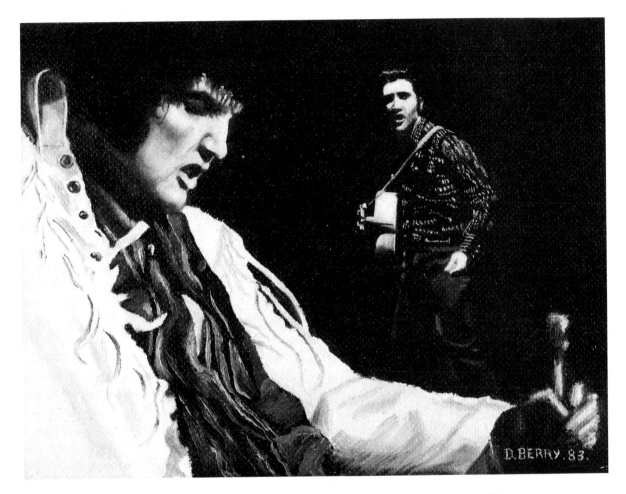

'In the early years, Elvis got burned by the country bumpkin label. The press seemed determined to make him look like Li'l Abner with money and he detested their efforts. Today, at 37, Elvis could give Mick Jagger a run for his money. For some reason he's dyed his hair even darker until it's blue-black. He's put rings on his fingers and bells on his boots. His suits are apt to be lapel-less – revealing a scarlet ruffled shirt with Napoleonic collar. His eyes are shaded by lavender wire-rim glasses with "Elvis" engraved on each side. He leans on a walking stick with a silver bulldog's head – with diamonds for eyes – as a handle. Inside it is a gun. The corn-pone accent is gone. The country boy image has vanished. His manners remain. But there is a taunting, challenging look in his eyes.'

Hollywood Magazine

Dennis Berry

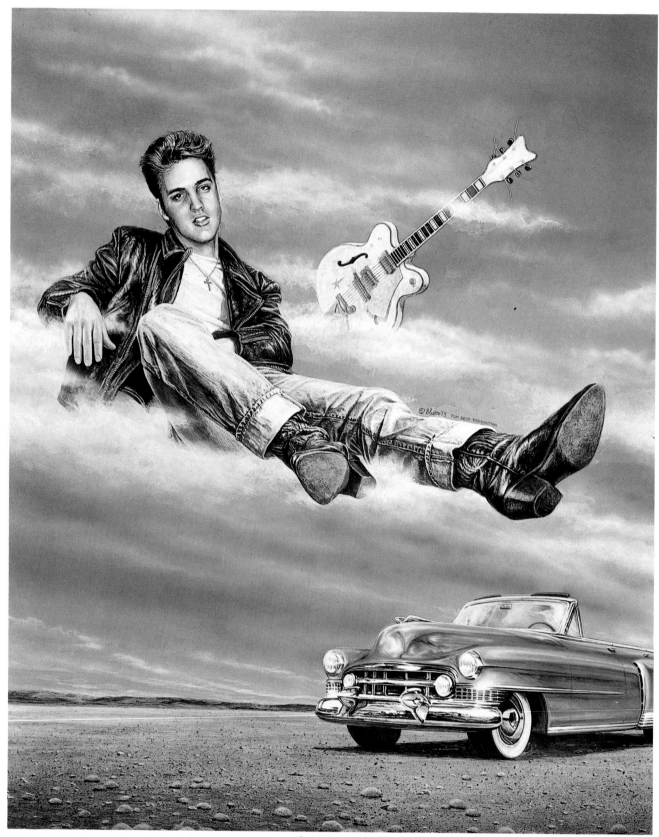

Gunter Blum

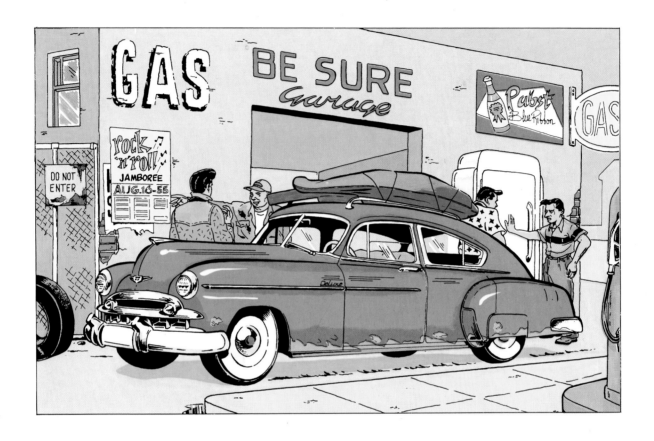

'Elvis loved this country like I do. Loved cars. Loved his daddy and his mama. And look how they done him.'

James Brown

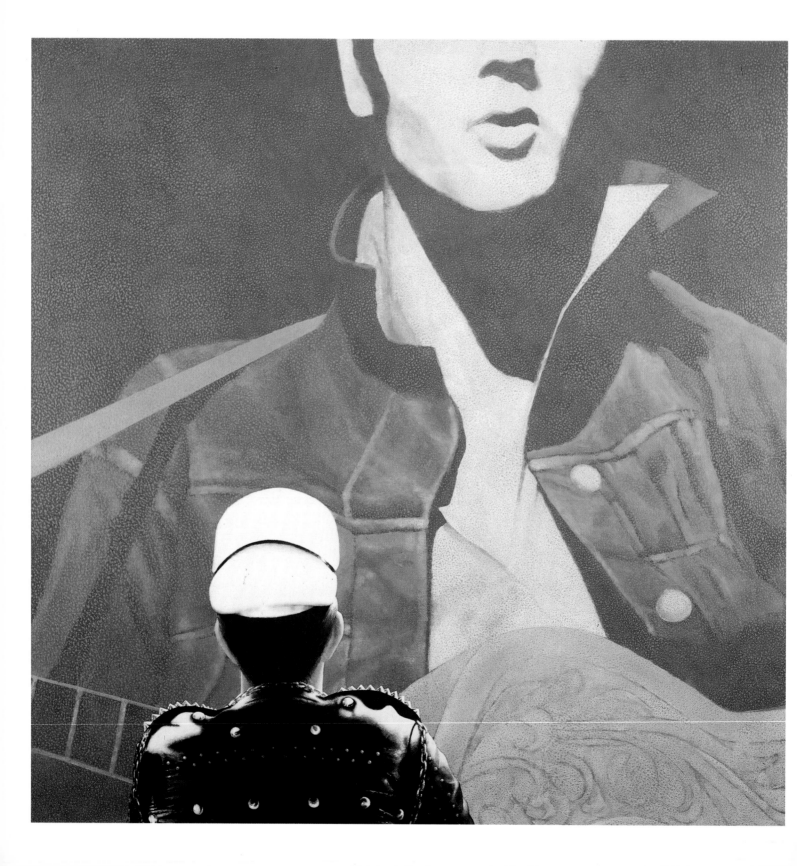

'Even back then, when people would laugh at his sideburns and his pink coat and call him 'cissy' — he had a pretty hard road to go. In some areas motorcycle gangs would come to the shows. They would come to get Elvis, but he never worried about it. He went right out and did his thing and before the show was over, they were standing in line to get his autograph too.'

Carl Perkins

David Oxtoby/Miki Slingsby Photography

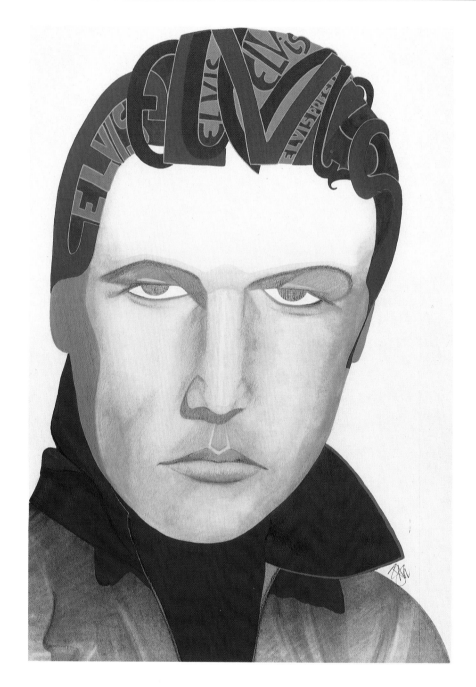

'He was a great, great man, and a very dear friend. I'm saddened, I can't believe it. I thought nothing could ever happen to him. It's like someone just came up and told me there aren't going to be any more cheeseburgers in the world.'

Felton Jarvis
(producer)

Joan (Batty Baines) Rudolph

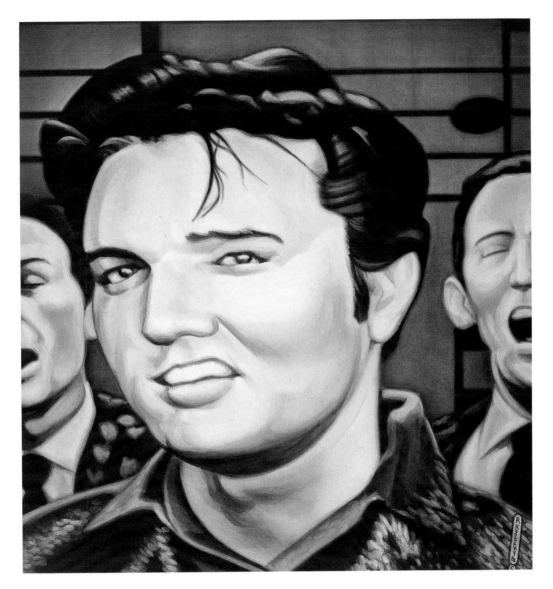

'Mr Presley made another television appearance last night on the Milton Berle show over Channel 4 . . . he might possibly be classified as an entertainer. Or, perhaps quite as easily as an assignment for a sociologist.'

Jack Gould
New York Times
7 June 1956

'The kid has no right behaving like a sex maniac on a national show.'

Jackie Gleason

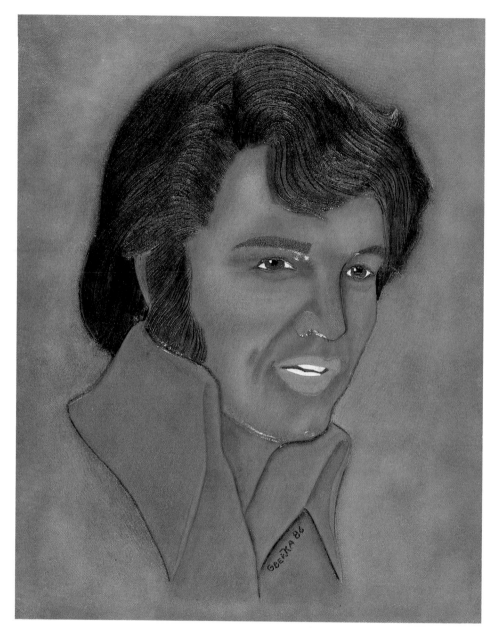

'I well remember my meeting with the Beatles and have recorded "Hey Jude" for my next album. They are so interesting and experimental, but I liked them particularly when they used to sing, "She Was Just Seventeen – You Know What I Mean!"'

Elvis Presley

George Berka: Hand-tooled in leather

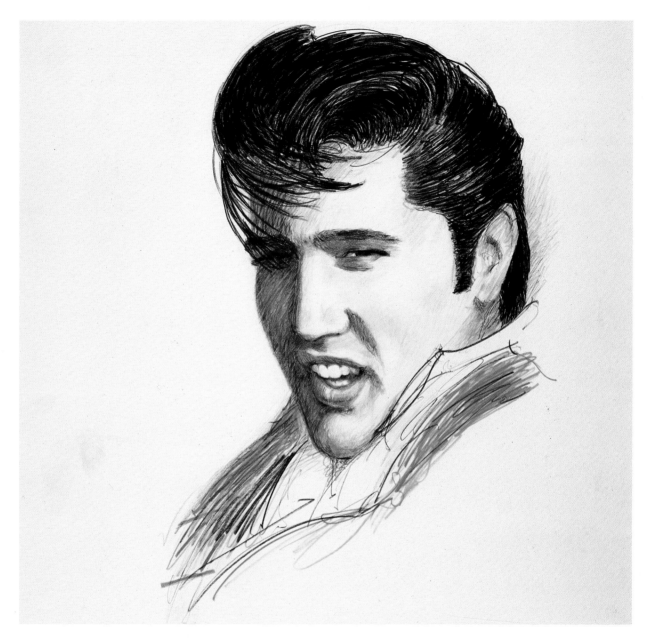

'He's the best-mannered star in Hollywood and he's improved as a performer and has a determination to be a fine actor. He was smart enough to simmer down that torrid act of his.'

Hedda Hopper

Steve La Rance

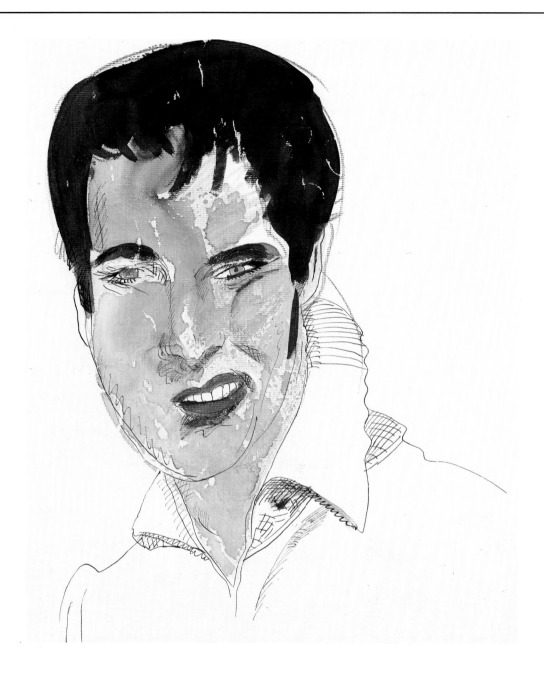

'Mr Presley has no discernible singing ability. His speciality is rhythm songs
which he renders in an undistinguished whine; his phrasing, if it can be
called that, consists of the stereotyped variations that go with a beginner's
aria in a bathtub. For the ear he is an unutterable bore . . .'

Jack Gould
New York Times
1956

Donna Muir

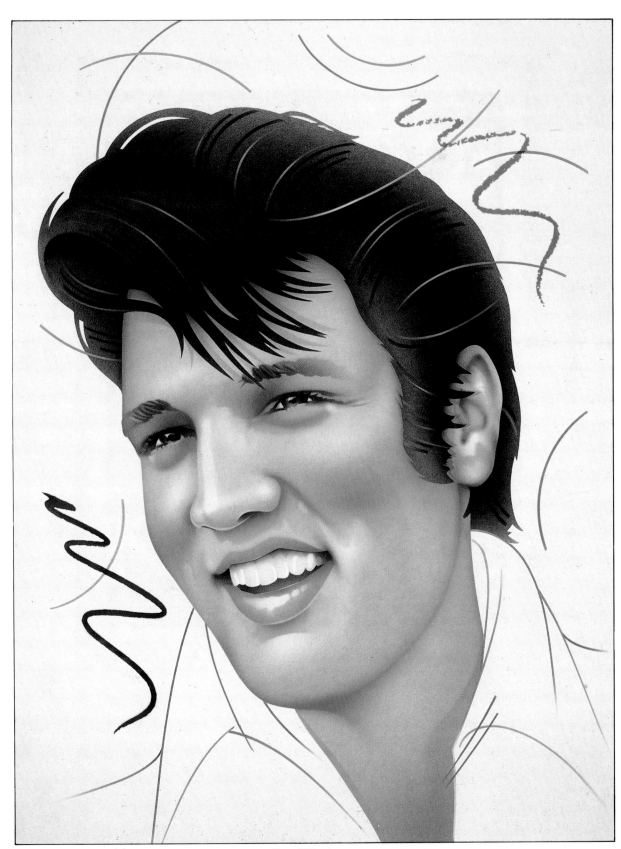

Dave Willardson

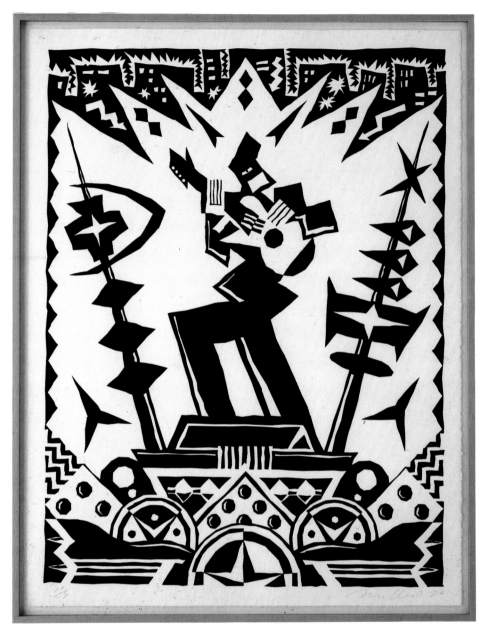

'Rock and Roll is the most brutal, ugly, degenerate, vicious form of expression – lewd, sly, in plain fact, dirty – a rancid-smelling aphrodisiac and the martial music of every side-burned delinquent on the face of the earth.'

Frank Sinatra

Tim Clark

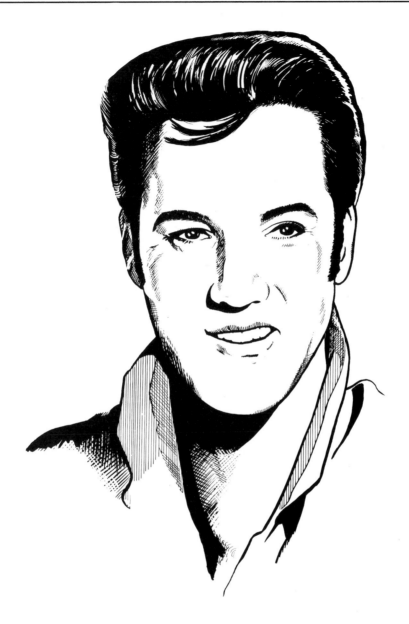

'I thought anyone who had been the centre of all that insanity for so long would have some of it rub off on him. But, after working in *Change of Habit* with him, I realised I'd never worked with a more gentlemanly, kinder man. He's gorgeous.'

Mary Tyler Moore

Alan Vince

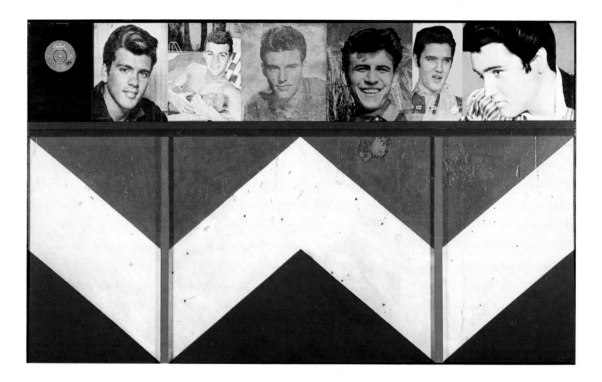

'Elvis will remain the founder of Rock and Roll in most people's minds, and every rock singer owes something to him in matter of inflection and visual style. The Beatles and Bob Dylan brought the music closer to art as it has been traditionally defined. But Elvis was and remained a working class hero, a man who rose from obscurity and transformed American popular art in answer to his own needs – and who may have possibly been destroyed by the isolation that being an American celebrity sometimes entails. He was as much a metaphor as a maker of music, and one of telling power and poignancy.'

John Rockwell
New York Times

Peter Blake: 'Got A Girl', courtesy of Whitworth Art Gallery, University of Manchester

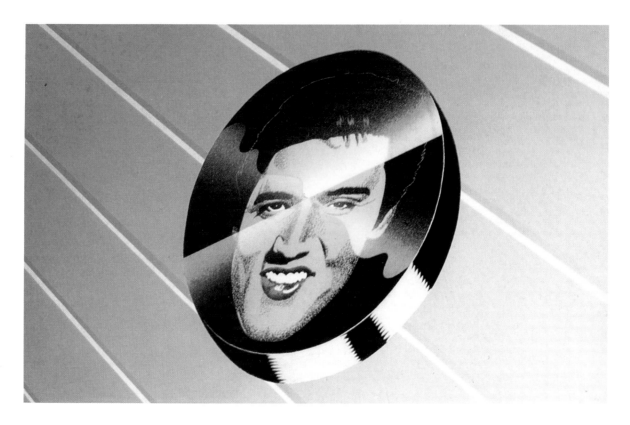

'The overwhelming nature of the arrival of Elvis Presley as a national figure
has tended to overshadow what should be the heart of the matter – his
music.'

John C Wilson
New York Times

'I think he's the greatest. I bought his records long before he was popular.
This boy's got a lot of voltage.'

Burl Ives

Lon Goddard: Detail of cover of 'Rock and Pop Brainbusters', published by Zomba Books

'He said he had a premonition that he would never live to be an old man because his mother had died fairly young, and that had a traumatic effect on him. He was not in the best of shape lately and he was very insecure. He told me he did not want to make another movie and he seemed to dread his public appearances. He had also gained a lot of weight which seemed to aggravate the situation, and he had a digestive problem of some kind. A lot of us wondered what an old Elvis Presley would be like. Now we will never know. He will always be the King . . . and no-one can take that away from him.'

Pat Boone

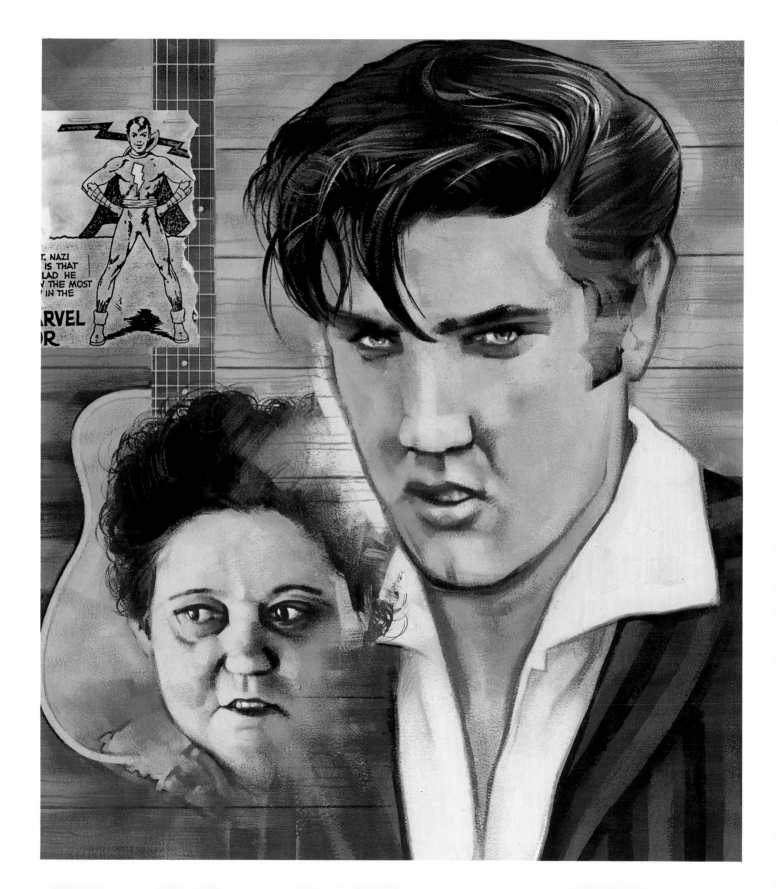

'People want to know why Ah can't stand still when Ah'm singin' . . . Some
people tap their feet, some people snap their fingers, some people just
sway back and forth . . . Ah just sorta do 'em all together, Ah guess. Singin'
rhythm and blues just really knocks it out. Ah watch my audience and
listen to 'em and Ah know that we're all gettin' somethin' out of our system
and none of us knows what it is . . . The important thing is we're all gettin' rid
of it and nobody's gettin' hurt . . .'

Elvis Presley

George Underwood

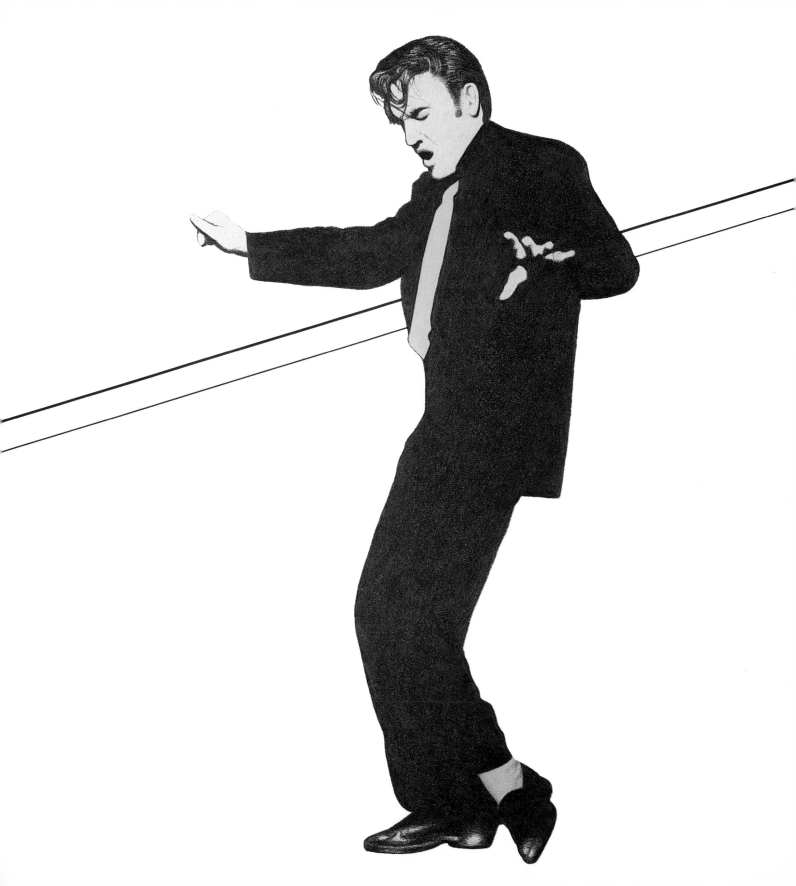

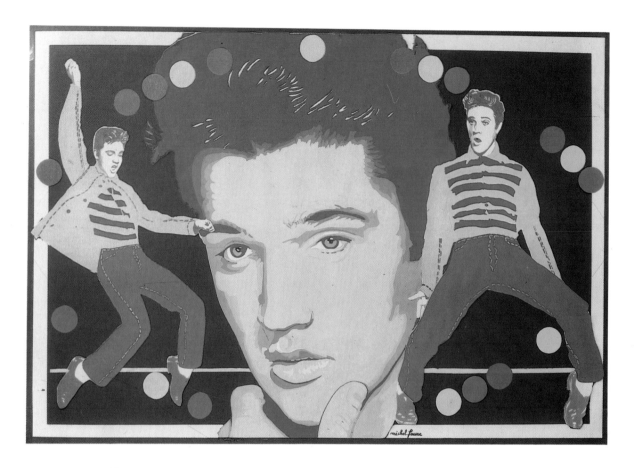

'Elvis who rotates his pelvis, is appalling musically. This fellow is supposed
to be a singer. But if his howling and yowling, wailing, screeching and
caterwauling is a form of song, then a tomcat on a back fence deserves
the title of 'world's greatest vocalist.' This new phenomenon, as he sings,
indulges in bumps and grinds and other motions that would bring a blush
to the cheeks of a hardened burlesque theater usher. He wiggles and
wriggles, itches and scratches, spins and gyrates as if he were doing a
loathesome takeoff of a victim of the St Vitus Dance.'

Ben Gross
New York Times

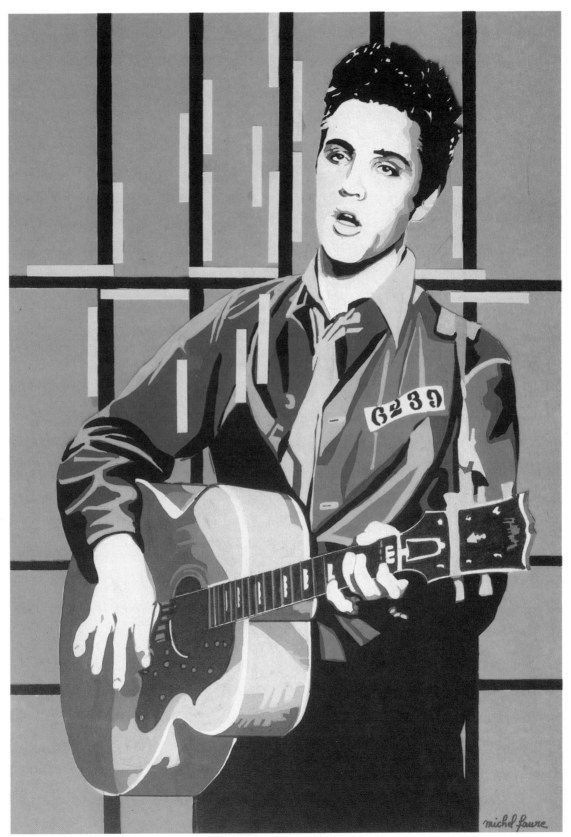

michel faure

'Is it a sausage? It is certainly smooth and damp looking, but whoever heard of a hundred and seventy-two pound sausage six foot tall? Is it a Walt Disney goldfish? It has the same sort of big, soft, beautiful eyes and long curly lashes, but whoever heard of a goldfish with sideburns? Is it a corpse? The fact it just hangs there, limp and white with its little drop-seat mouth, rather like Lord Byron in the wax museum . . . but suddenly the figure comes to life.'

Time Magazine

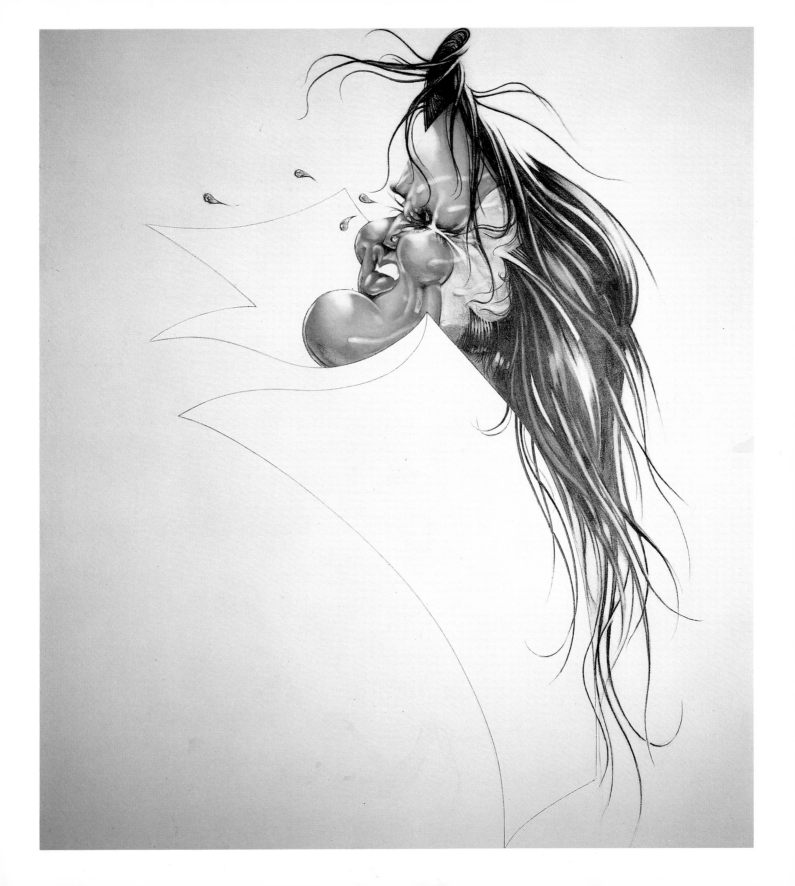

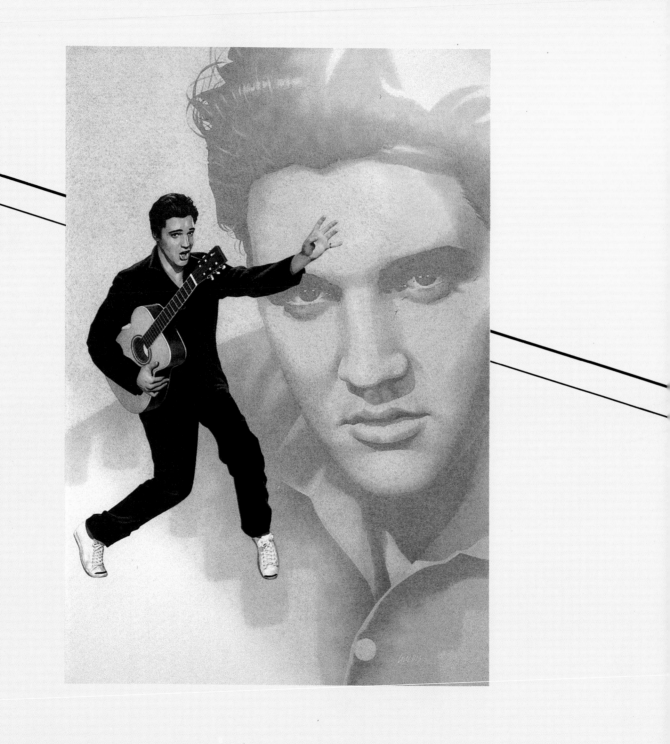

'A lot of people used to put Elvis down, say he held the guitar like a prop, but he could make his way through all right, and he could play piano a bit too. When we played together, in fact, I was surprised at how much he did know. But the real thing was his way of crying out a lyric in a song – it was the same with Otis.'

Steve Cropper
(guitarist)

'I remember that when my father told us he was being sent to Wiesbaden
Air Base, I mentioned jokingly that Elvis Presley was stationed nearby and
maybe we would get a chance to meet him. My mother said, "I wouldn't
let you walk across the street to see Elvis Presley."'

Priscilla Presley

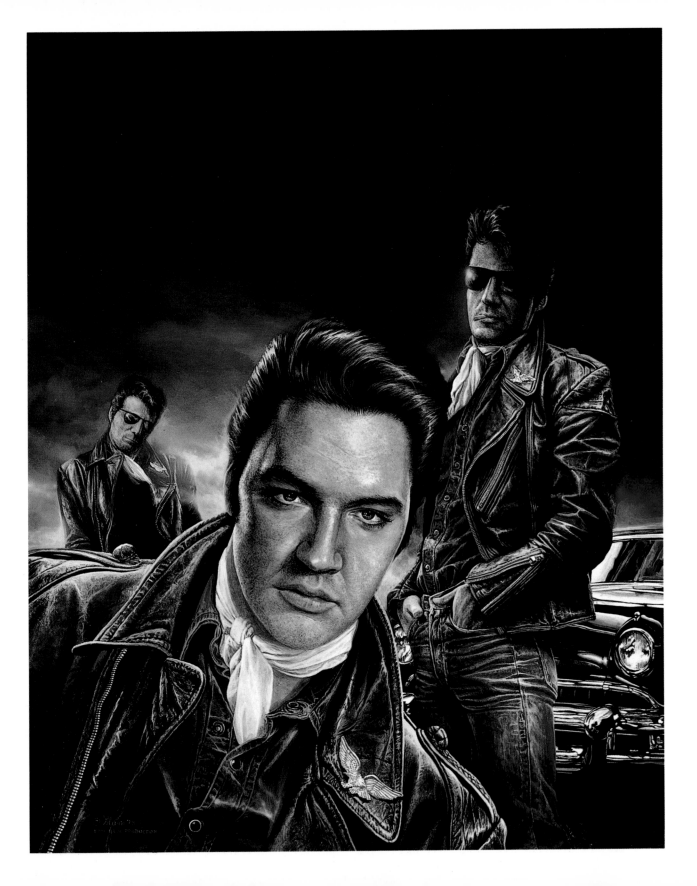

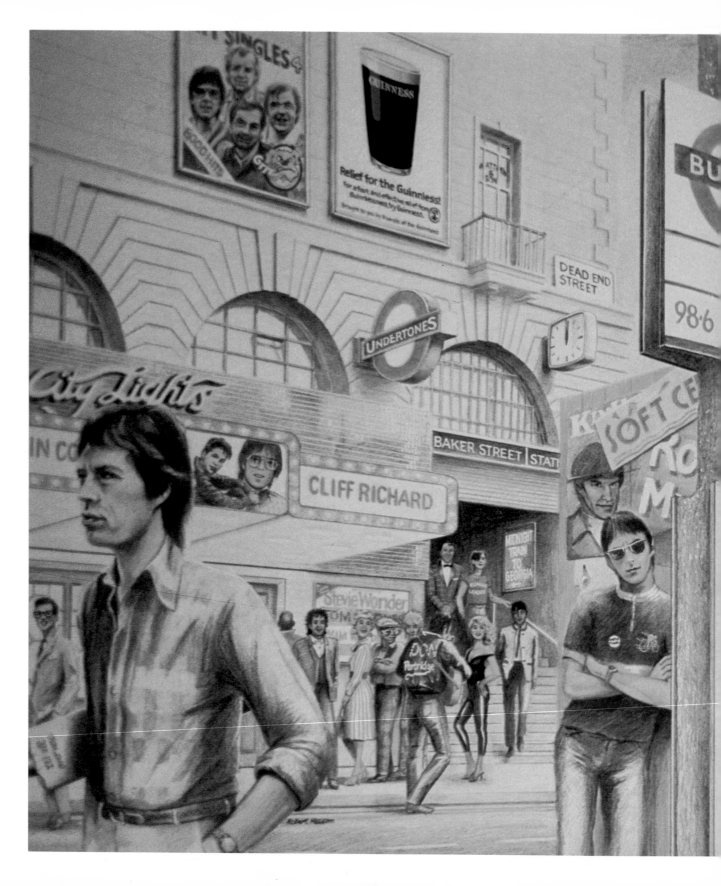

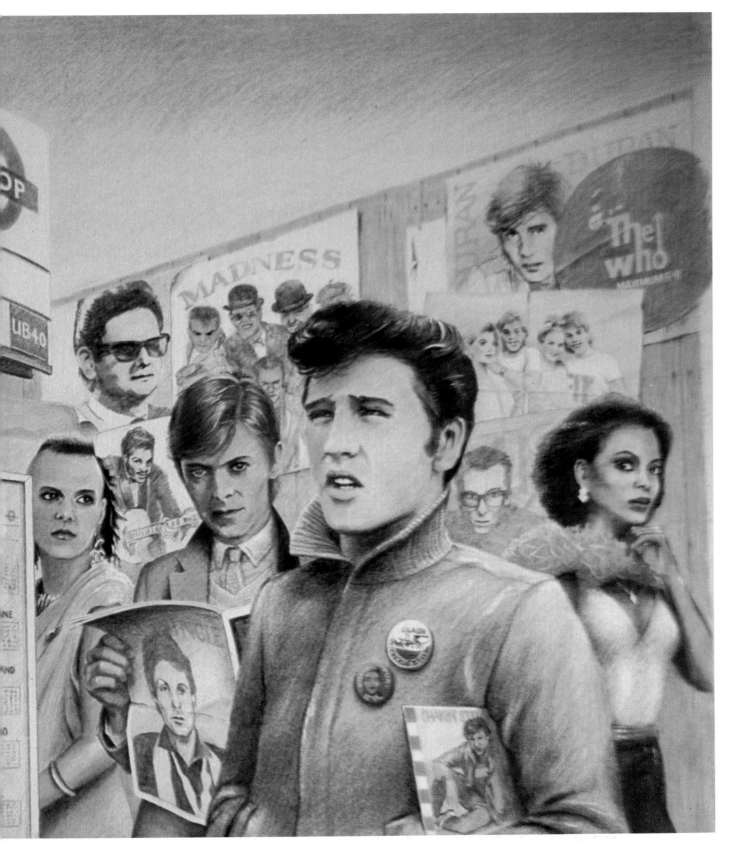

Detail from the jacket of the Guinness Book of British Hit Singles [4th edition]. Artist: Robert Heesom, Art Editor: David Roberts

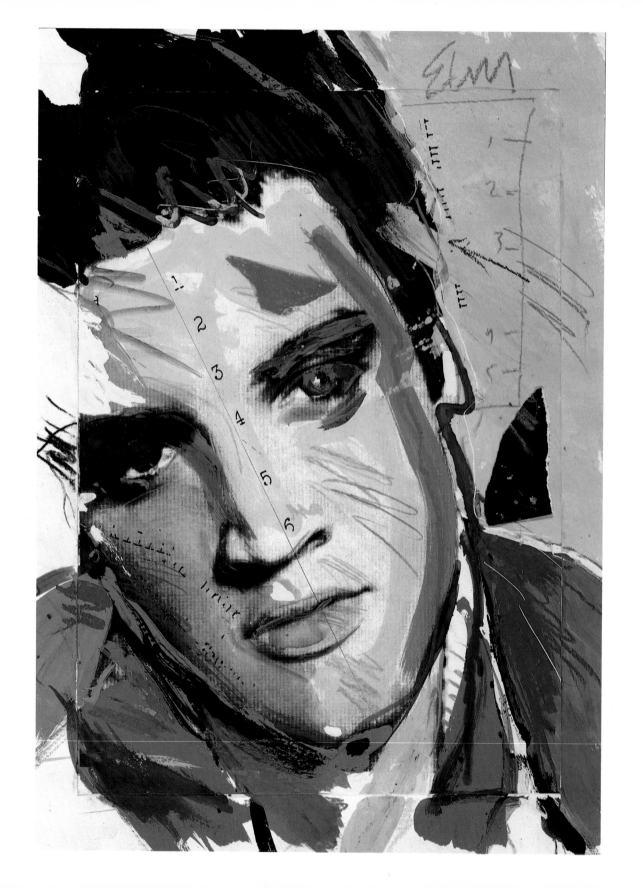

'I was a real little toddler when I first heard 'Hound Dog'. I learned to play drums listening to him – beating on tin cans to his records. I'm sure his measurable effect on culture and music was even greater in England than in the States. People there are still really, really fanatical about Elvis. The news came over like a ton of bricks. I was driving back from the mountains and I had the radio on. They were playing an Elvis medley and I thought "Great." And then they came back with the news.'

Mick Fleetwood

'Elvis has said, "I want to make one with Satch." You'd be surprised what we could do together.'

Louis Armstrong

'When Presley injected movements of the tongue and indulged in wordless singing, that was singularly distasteful on the Sullivan show; enough was enough. When Presley executes his bumps and grind, it must be remembered by the Columbia Broadcasting system that even the twelve-year-olds' curiosity may be over-stimulated. In the long run perhaps Presley will do everyone a favour by pointing up the need for early sex education so that neither his successors nor TV can capitalize on the idea that his type of routine is somehow highly tempting, yet forbidden fruit.'

Jack Gould
New York Times

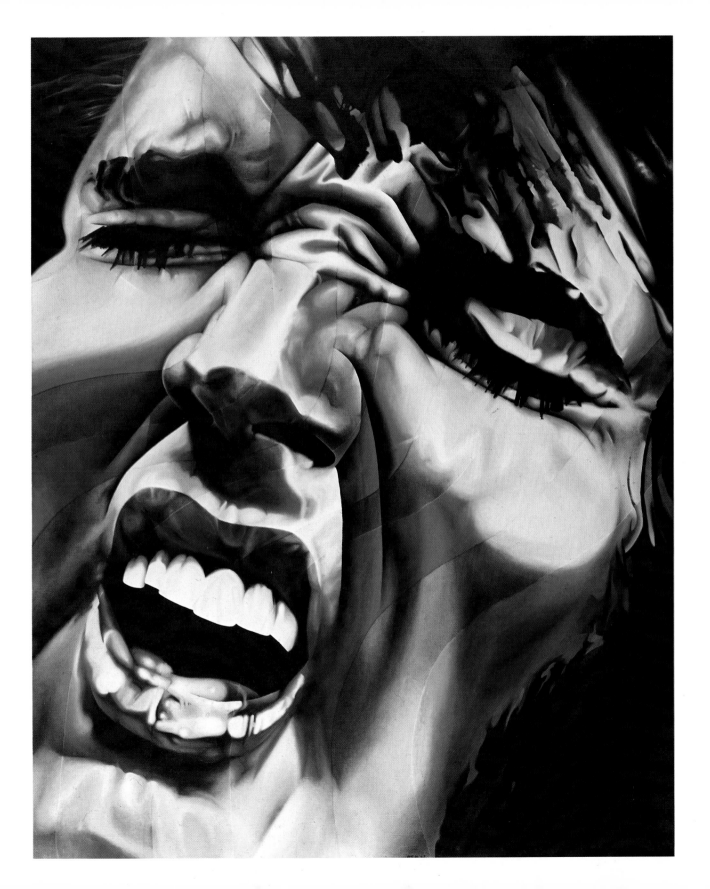

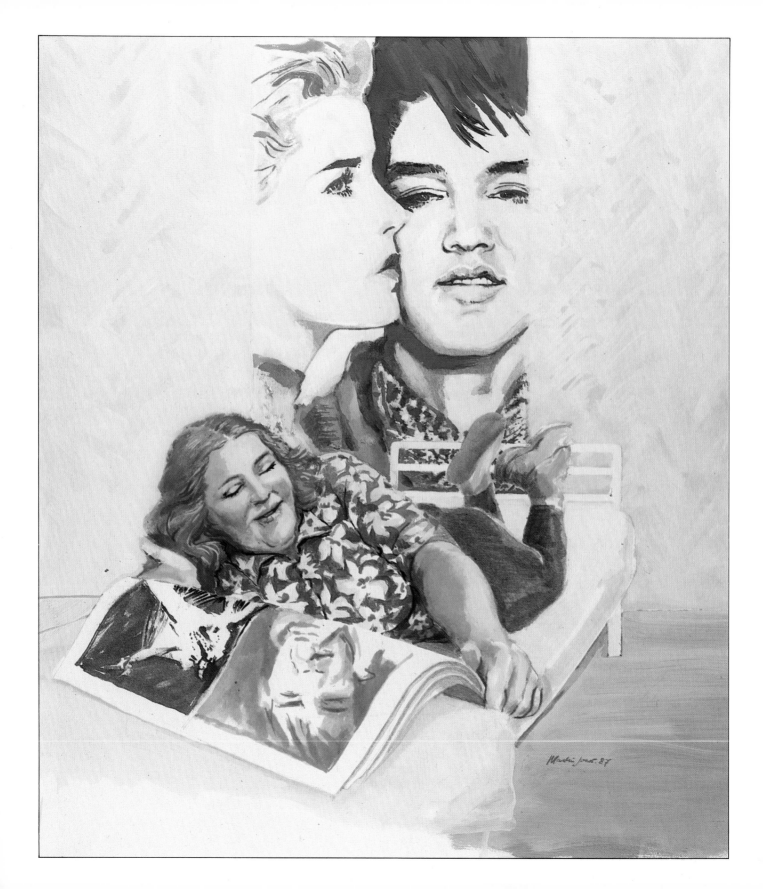

'As for the fans, they've changed some but they're still there, the same ones. The president of one fan club came to see me and I hardly recognized her. She's going to college now. I was surprised she looked me up. She was more mature, but she stopped by anyway.'

Elvis Presley
in *Newsweek*

'Elvis loved gospel music. He was raised on it. And he really did know what he was talking about. He was singing gospel all the time – almost anything he did had that flavour anyhow. At least I heard it. You can't get away from what your roots are.'

Cissy Houston

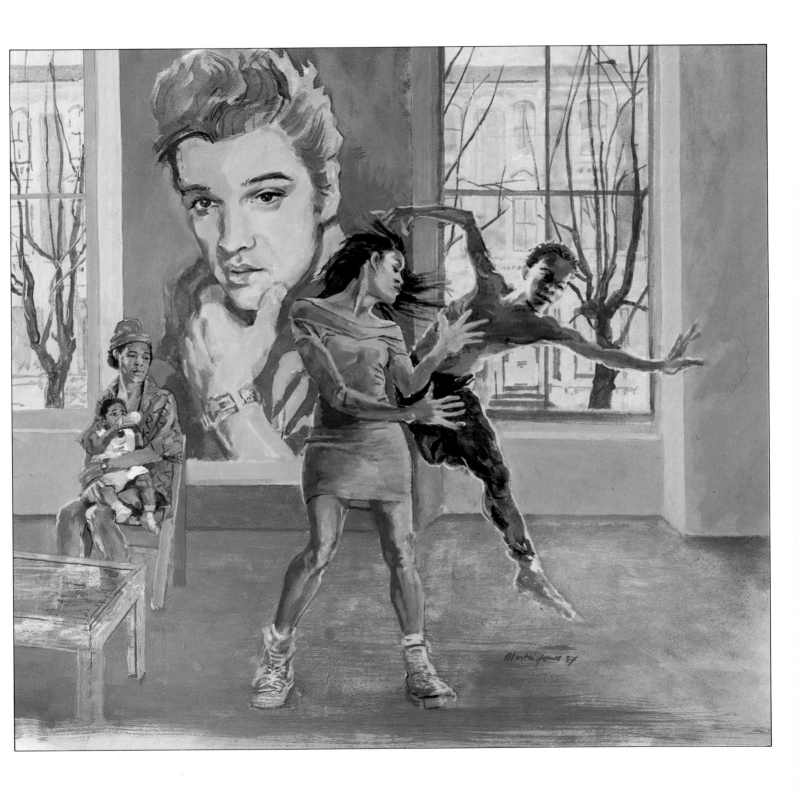

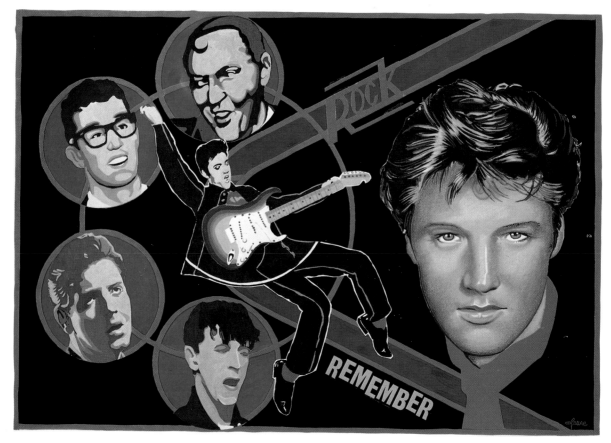

'His death is really the end of a beginning. Anyone who has ever thought of entering the pop business could not possibly have failed to be influenced by Elvis. I honestly think that there has never been a person in the pop world like him.'

Adam Faith

'I hadn't been around anyone who was religious. He felt he had been given this gift, this talent, by God. He didn't take it for granted. He thought it was something that he had to protect. He had to be nice to people, otherwise God would take it all away.'

Natalie Wood

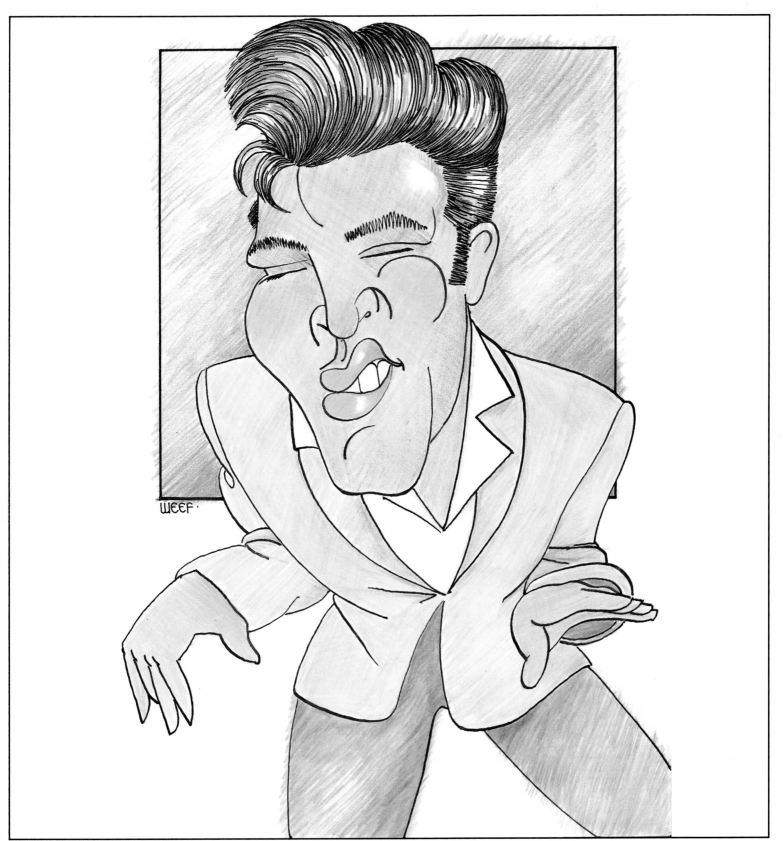

Weef

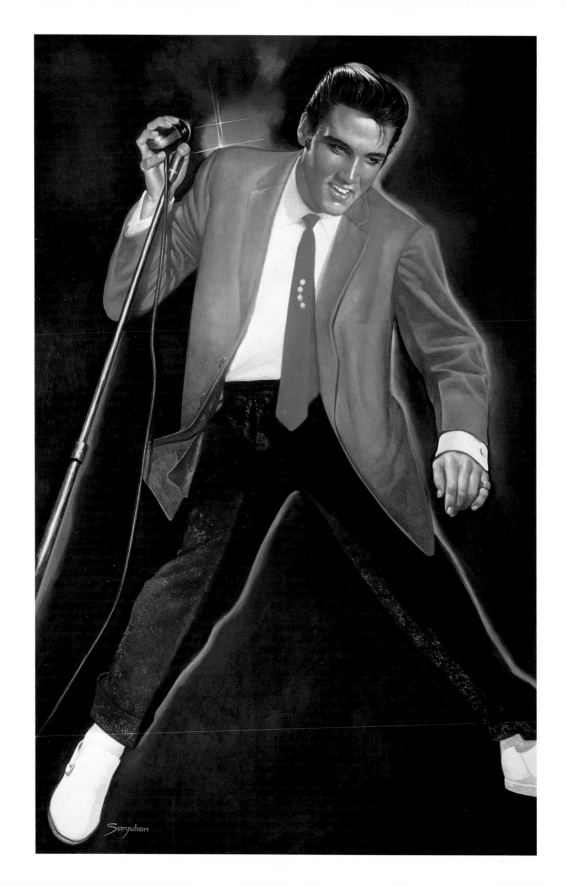

'From watching Mr Presley it is wholly evident that his skill lies in another direction. He is a rock-and-roll variation of one of the most standard acts in show business: the virtuoso of the hootchy-kootchy. His one speciality is an accented movement of the body that heretofore has been primarily identified with the repertoire of the blonde bombshells of the burlesque runway. The gyration never had anything to do with the world of popular music and still doesn't.'

Jack Gould
New York Times
1956

'It's really simple, but no one seems to understand it. When I was a boy, I used to think that sideburns and a moustache would make me look older. I couldn't grow the moustache, so I settled for sideburns.'

Elvis Presley

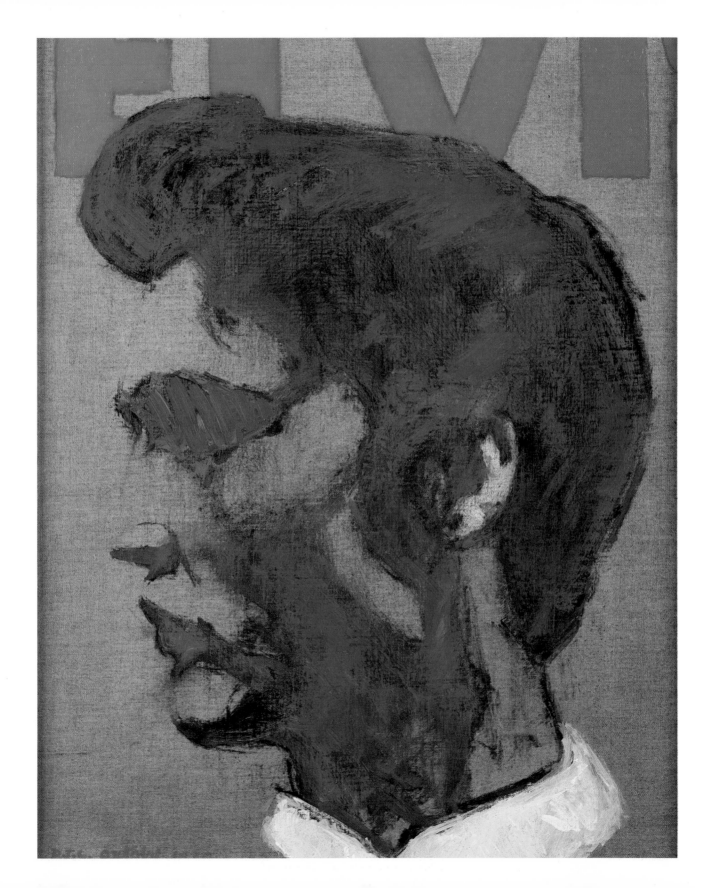

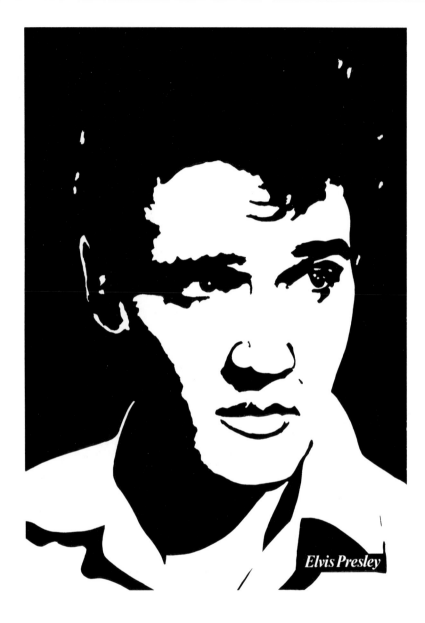

Elvis Presley

'I'm ambitious to become a more serious actor, but I don't want to give up
the music business by no means. I can't change my style either. If I feel like
moving around, I still move.'

Elvis Presley

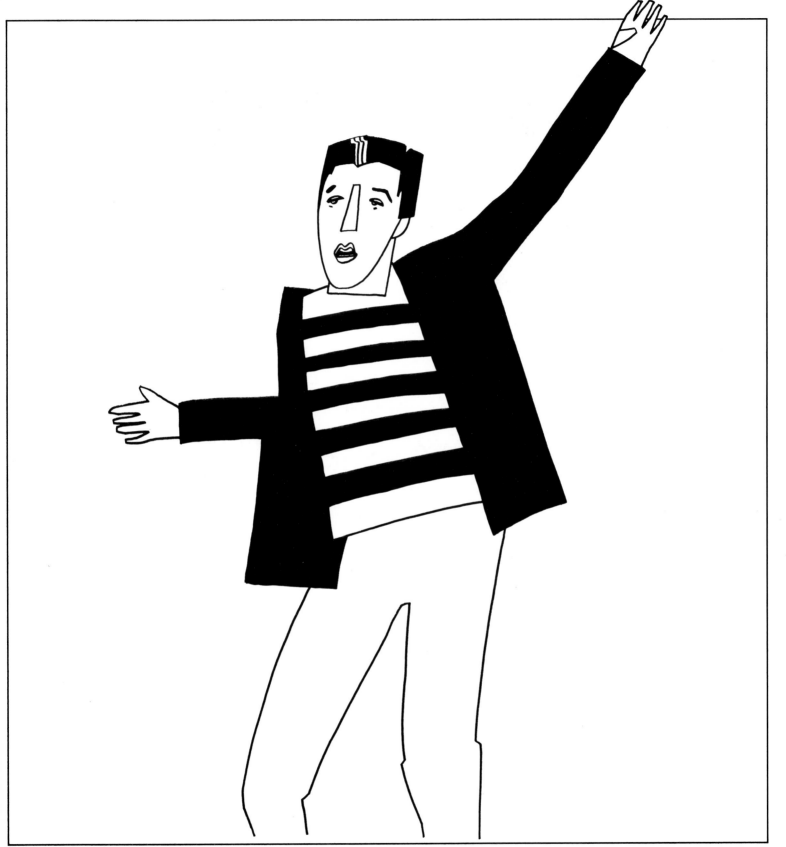

David Reeson

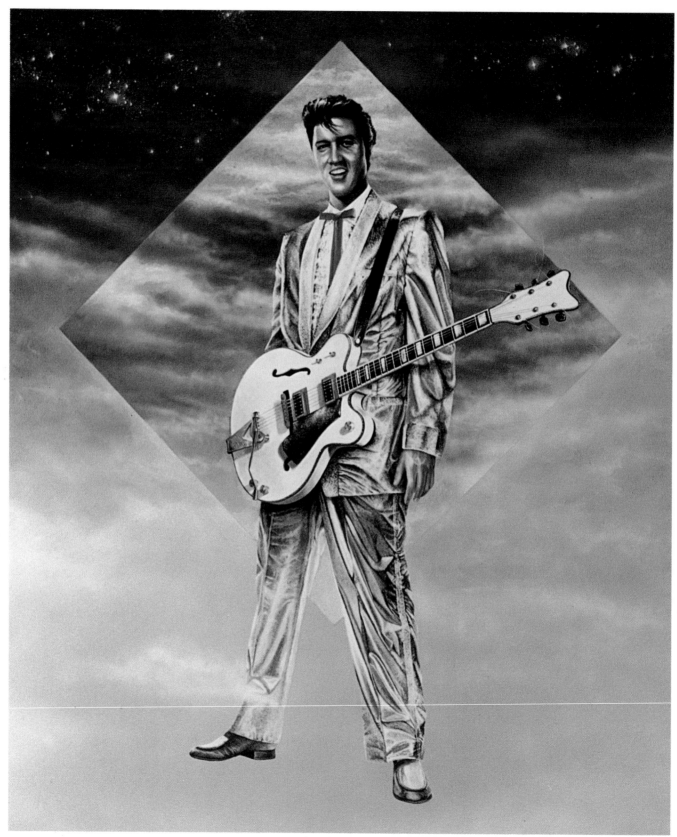

Gunter Blum

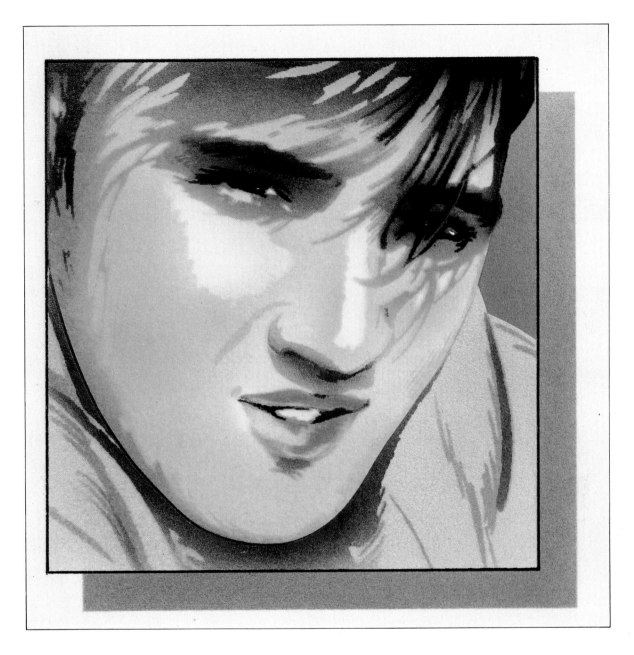

'God must have been impatient for some rock'n'roll in heaven.'

Jimmy Saville

Dave Willardson

'The first time I heard his music, back in '54 or '55, I was in a car and I heard the announcer say, "Here's a guy who, when he appears on stage in the South, the girls scream and rush the stage". Then he played 'That's All Right, Mama'. I thought his name was about the weirdest I'd ever heard. I thought for sure he was a Black guy. Later on I grew my hair like him, imitated his stage act – once I went all over New York looking for a lavender shirt like the one he wore on one of his albums. I felt wonderful when he sang 'Bridge Over Troubled Water', even though it was a touch on the dramatic side – but so was the song.'

Paul Simon

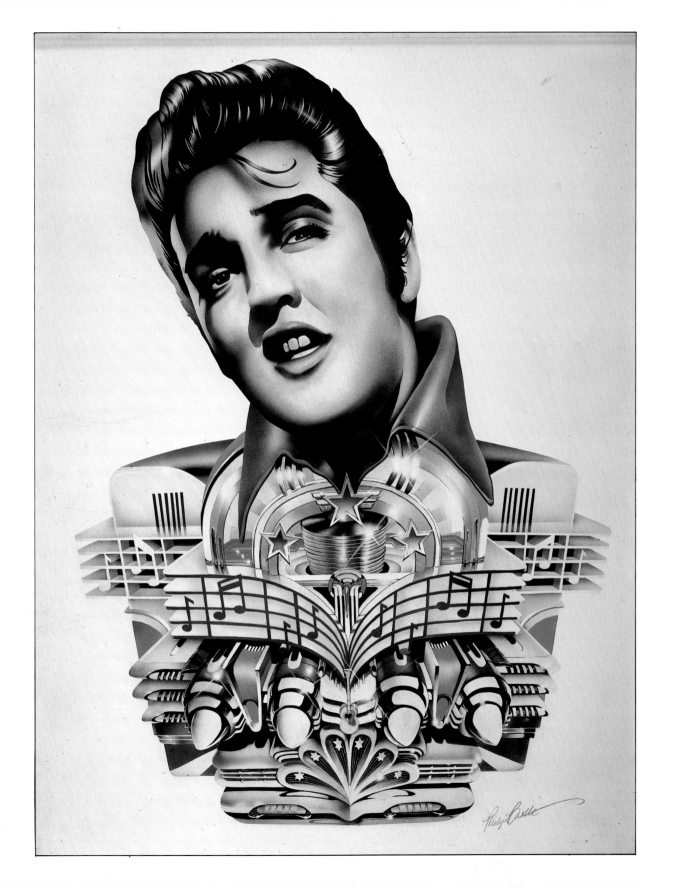

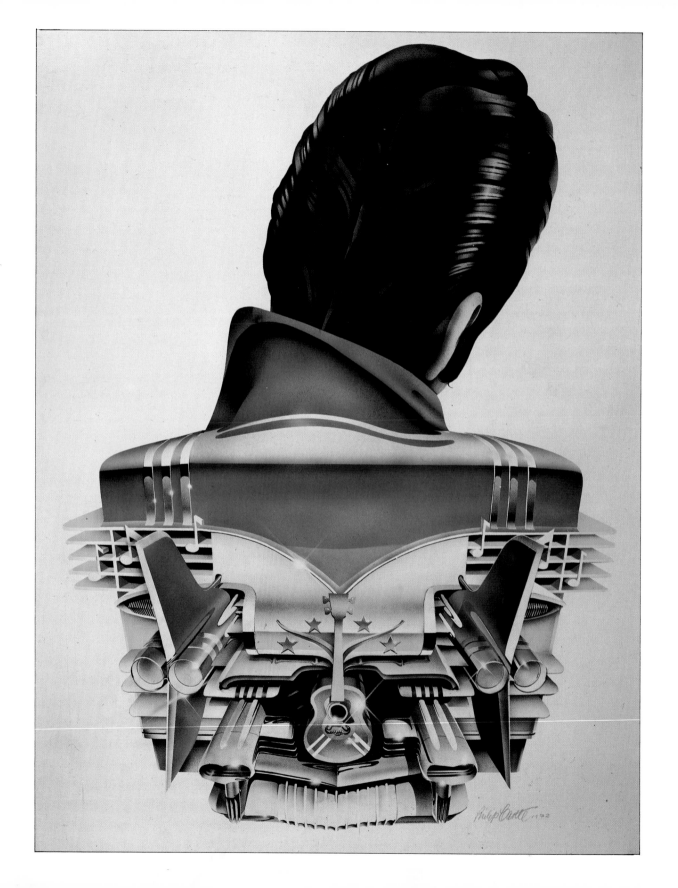

'People have said my absence from personal appearances has given the Beatles their big opportunities. I know nothing about that. I'll say the Beatles have got what it takes and in great abundance and that they've been given a heck of a vote of confidence.'

Elvis Presley

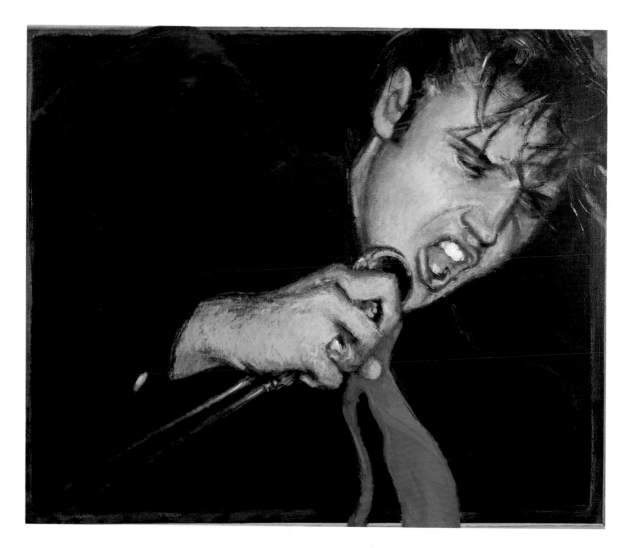

'The hair was a vaseline cathedral, the mouth a touchingly uncertain sneer of allure. One, two-wham! Like a berserk blender the lusty young pelvis whirred and the notorious git-tar slammed forward with a jolt that symbolically deflowered a generation of teenagers and knocked chips off 90 million older shoulders. Then out of the half-melted vanilla face a wild black baritone came bawling in orgasmic lurches. *Whu-huh-huh-hun f'the money! Two f'the show! Three t'git riddy naa GO CAAT GO!*'

Brad Darrach
Life
Winter 1977

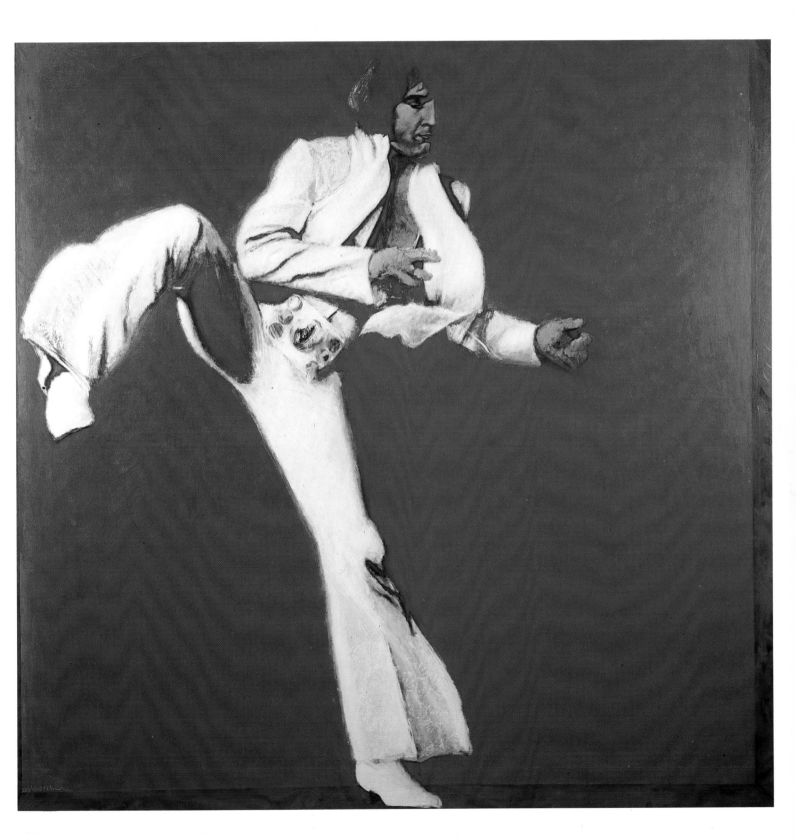

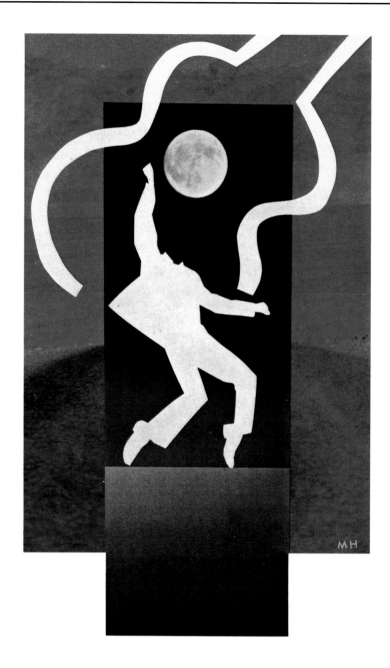

'The key phrases are pressure from other people, investments
mushrooming and dying strangely.'

Antonia Lamb
Horoscope forecast prepared for Elvis in 1970

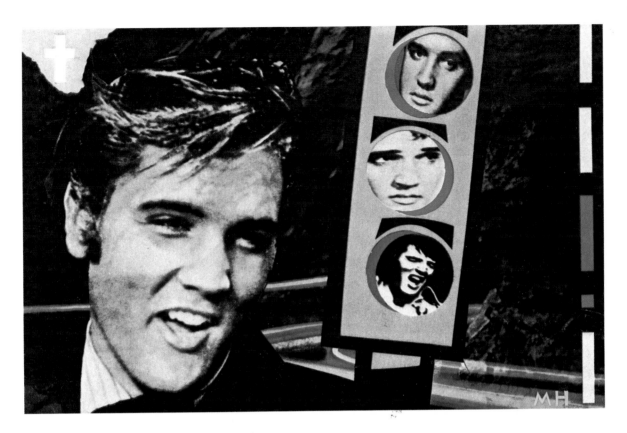

'How tragic that the once handsome face blew up like a balloon along with the rest of his body, due to a daily overdose of pills and drugs.'

Diana Dors

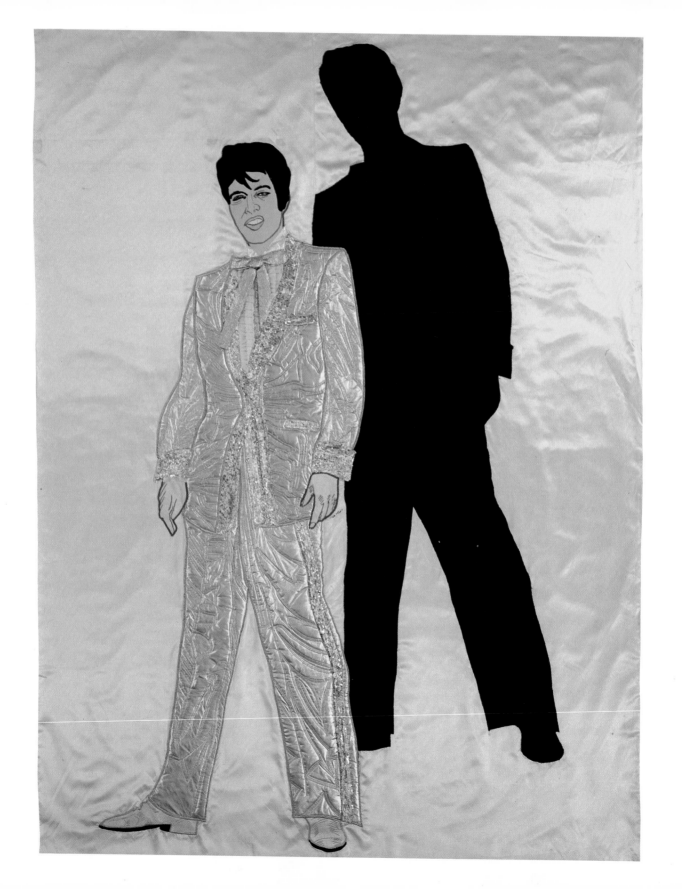

'A truly good man who never forgot his friends or his fans.'

Liberace

'When I first knew Elvis he had a million dollars worth of talent. Now he has
a million dollars.'

Colonel Tom Parker

'It was a real thrill sitting there with the King. I mean he was always one of my favourites. I always knew that no matter how I felt, if I played an Elvis record it would make me happy. I've always dreamed of producing an album for Elvis.'

Paul McCartney

'There's only one person in the United States that we have ever wanted to meet . . . not that he wanted to meet us. And we met him last night. We can't tell you how we felt. We just idolized him so much. When we first came to town, these guys like Dean Martin and Frank Sinatra and all these people wanted to come over and hang around with us at night simply because we had all the women, all the chicks. We don't want to meet those people. They don't really like us. We don't really admire or like them. The only person that we wanted to meet in the United States of America was Elvis Presley. We can't tell you what a thrill that was last night.'

John Lennon

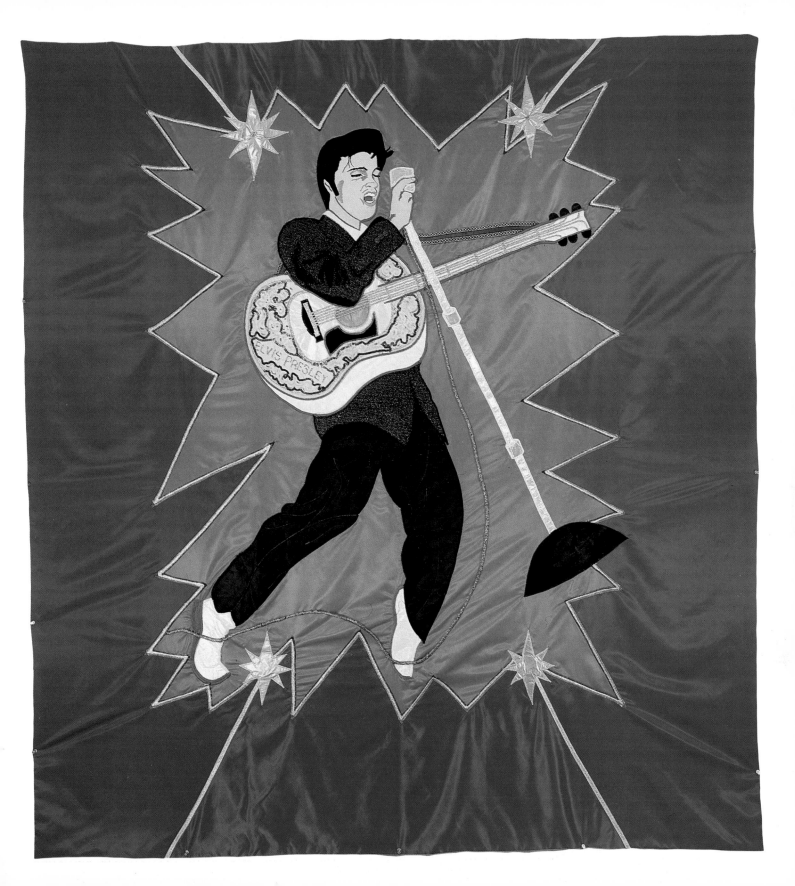

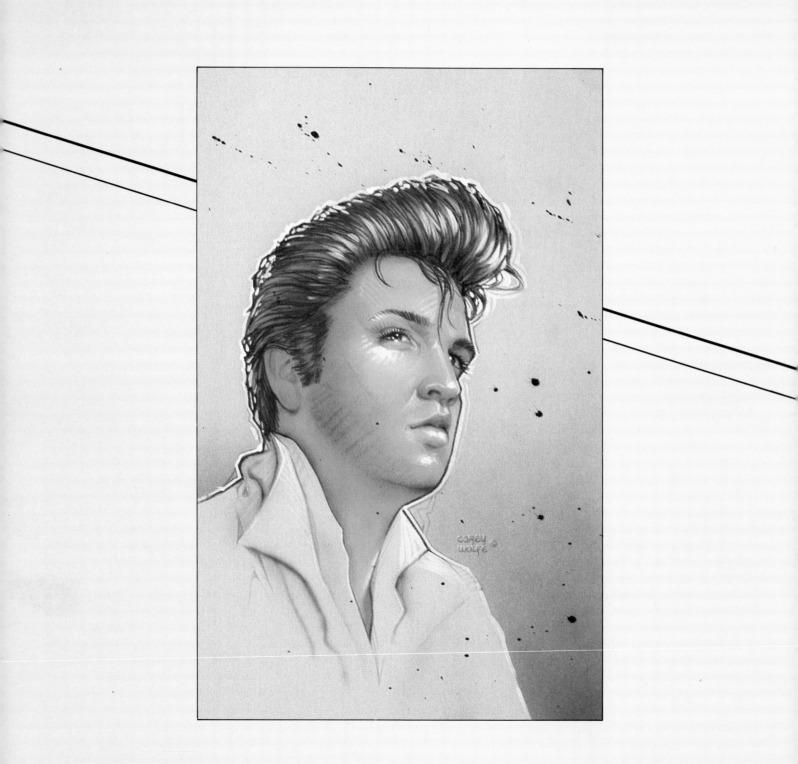

'For my so-called date with Elvis, I didn't dress up because I still didn't believe it. Next thing I knew I was on my way to Elvis's house, which he shared with his father. Elvis was sitting when I arrived. He got up and shook my hand. Then reality hit me. I thought, "What am I doing here?"'

Priscilla Presley

'His proposal was without ceremony. One day he simply showed me the ring and asked me to marry him. Elvis put a three-carat diamond ring on my finger. The little diamonds went all the way round. With the Colonel's usual help and excellent organization, we gave a reception for the press and Elvis's business friends. Then El and I took the next plane to Palm Springs, where we spent the next four days in bed.'

Priscilla Presley

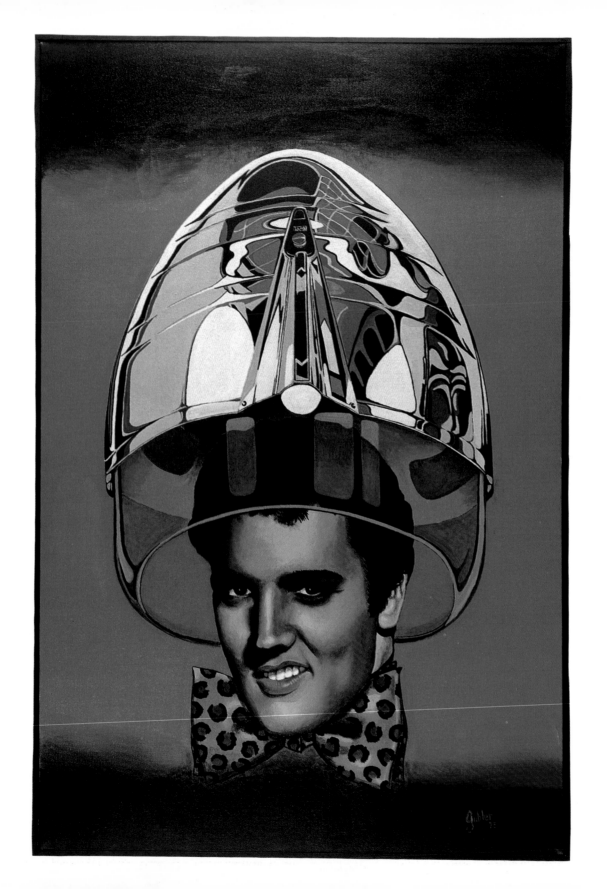

'If any man was born with everything it takes to become a superstar in the way of looks, talent and sex appeal, Elvis had the proverbial silver spoon in his mouth. He also managed to put a great deal more in that same mouth, which had rocked and shaken us all with a whole new concept of music way back in the fabulous 50's – and I do not just mean an assortment of junk food that would give most of us a heart attack.'

Diana Dors

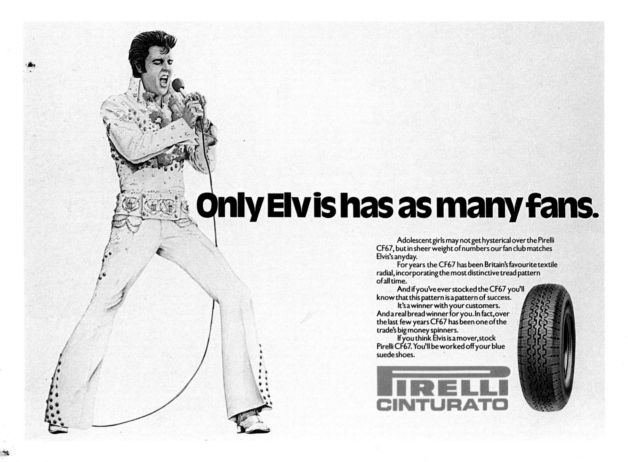

Only Elvis has as many fans.

Adolescent girls may not get hysterical over the Pirelli CF67, but in sheer weight of numbers our fan club matches Elvis's any day.

For years the CF67 has been Britain's favourite textile radial, incorporating the most distinctive tread pattern of all time.

And if you've ever stocked the CF67 you'll know that this pattern is a pattern of success.

It's a winner with your customers. And a real bread winner for you. In fact, over the last few years CF67 has been one of the trade's big money spinners.

If you think Elvis is a mover, stock Pirelli CF67. You'll be worked off your blue suede shoes.

PIRELLI CINTURATO

'What a frenzy this boy can stir up! I've never seen anything like it. When Elvis sings it isn't just a case of girls sighing and going swoony or stamping and shouting. I saw him send five thousand of them into a mass of screaming hysterics.'

Daily Mirror

'I was on the show (at Overton Park, Memphis) as an extra added single . . . and I came out on stage and I was scared stiff. My first big appearance, in front of an audience. And I came out and I was doin' a fast tune, uh, one of my first records, and everybody was hollerin' and I didn't know what they was hollerin' at. Everybody was screamin' and everything, and I came off stage and my manager told me they were hollerin' because I was wigglin'. Well I went back out for an encore and I kind-a did a little more and the more I did, the wilder they went.'

Elvis Presley

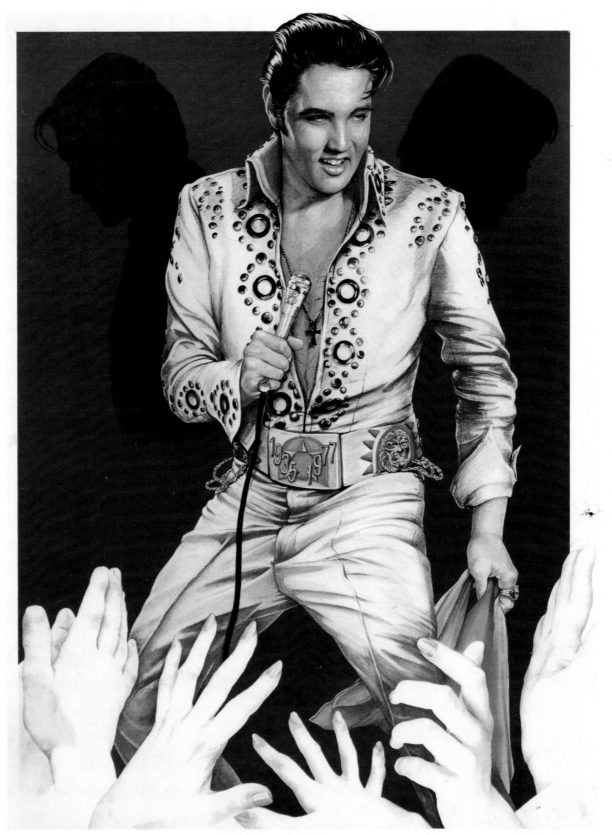

© Kathy Wyatt

'Zoom in on his undulating lips, curled in a demi-sneer, suggestive curl. His snake eyes gleam smugly; he is the total package, a cunning man cunningly manipulated to the top.'

Jonathan Eisen

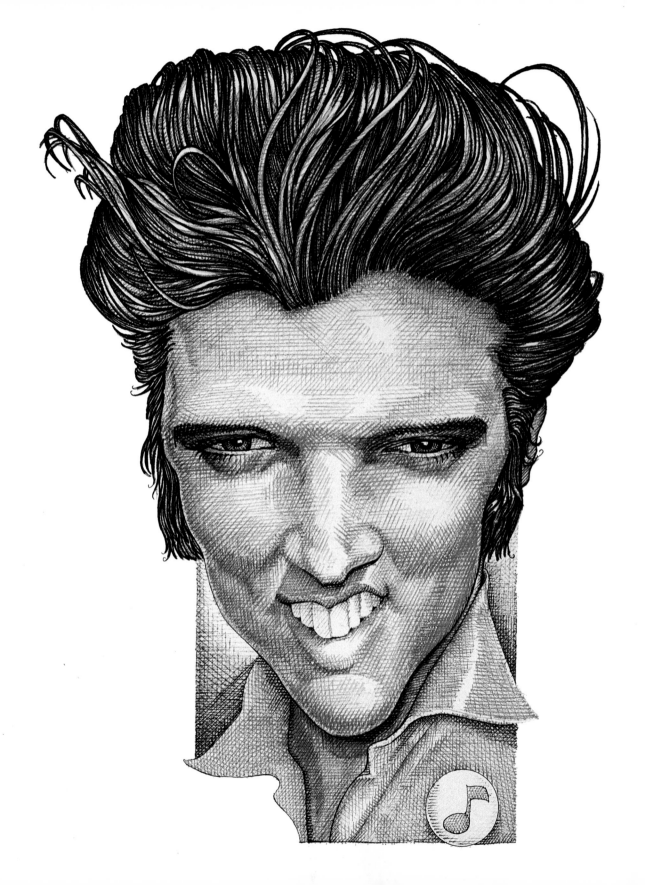

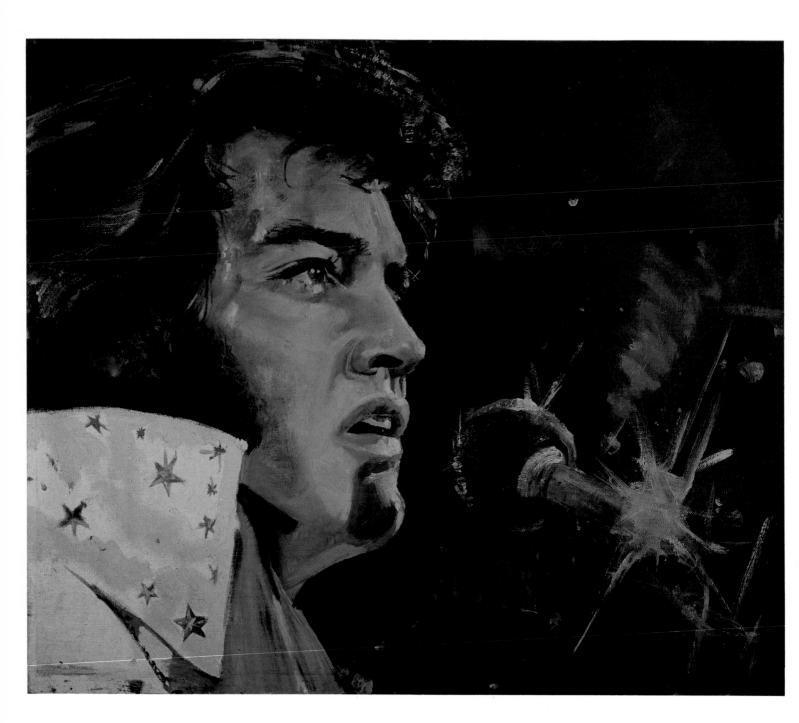

'I never wanted to become like Elvis – not through financial greed anyway. I don't want to become a fat, rich, sick, reclusive rock star. I want to continue as I've always done. I don't want to die.'

Johnny Rotten

'It's Elvis at his most indifferent, uninterested and unappealing. He's not just a little out of shape, not just a bit chubbier than usual, the living legend is fat and ludicrously aping his former self. It is a tragedy, disheartening and absolutely depressing to see Elvis in such diminishing stature.'

Hollywood reporter

'Ever since he came along we've been losing our identities. There used to be pop *and* gospel *and* country and so on. Now they're all fusing together. You can hardly tell the difference between a James Taylor record and a Waylon Jennings record.'

Chet Atkins

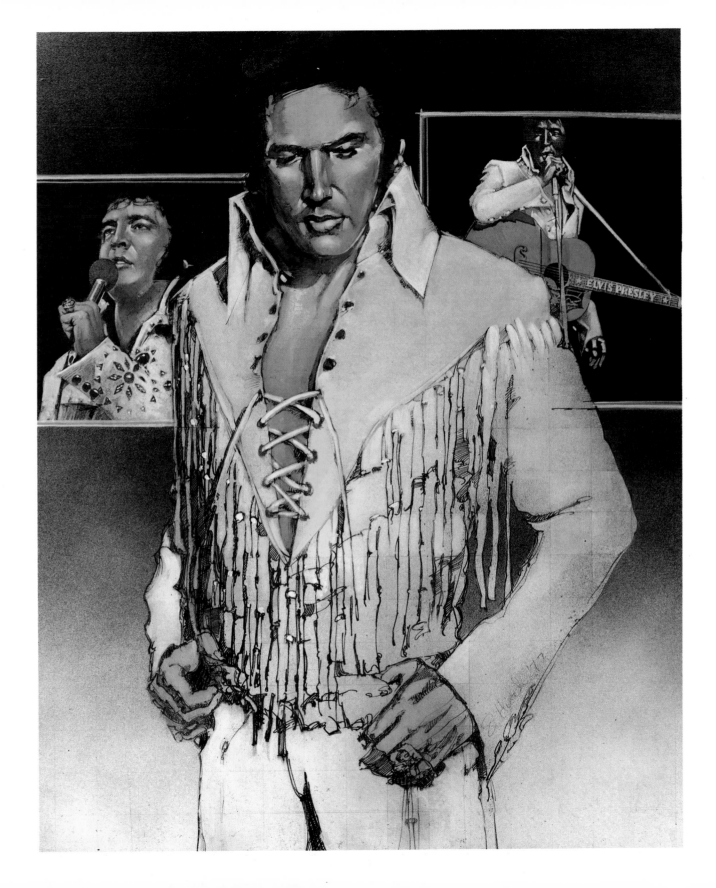

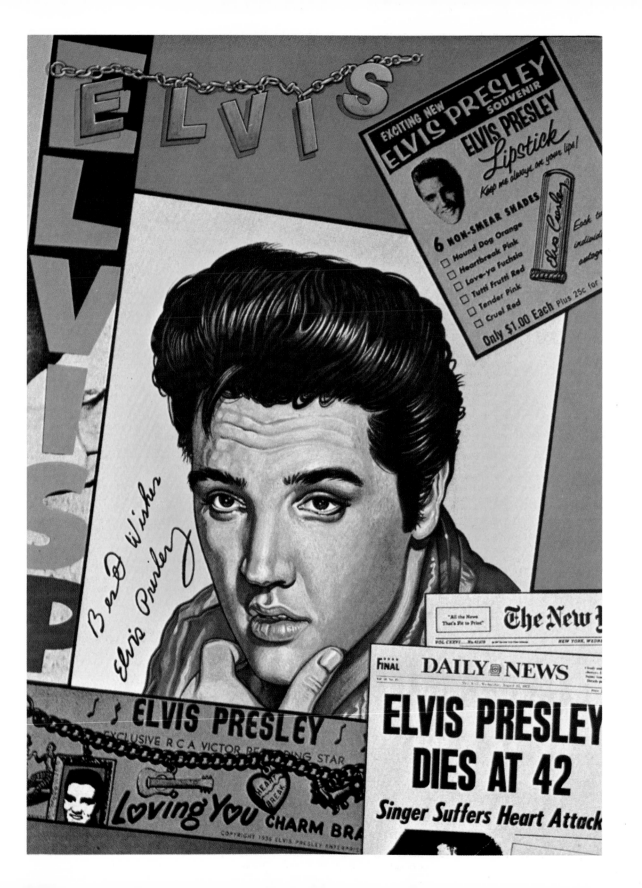

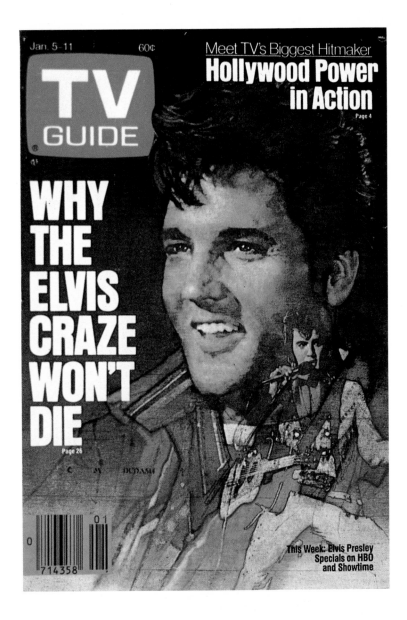

'Nothing really affected me until I heard Elvis. If there hadn't been an Elvis, there wouldn't have been the Beatles.'

John Lennon

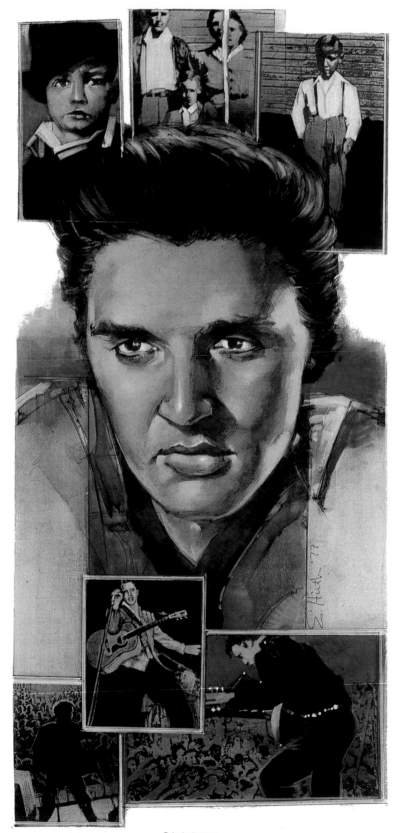

Edwin B. Hirth

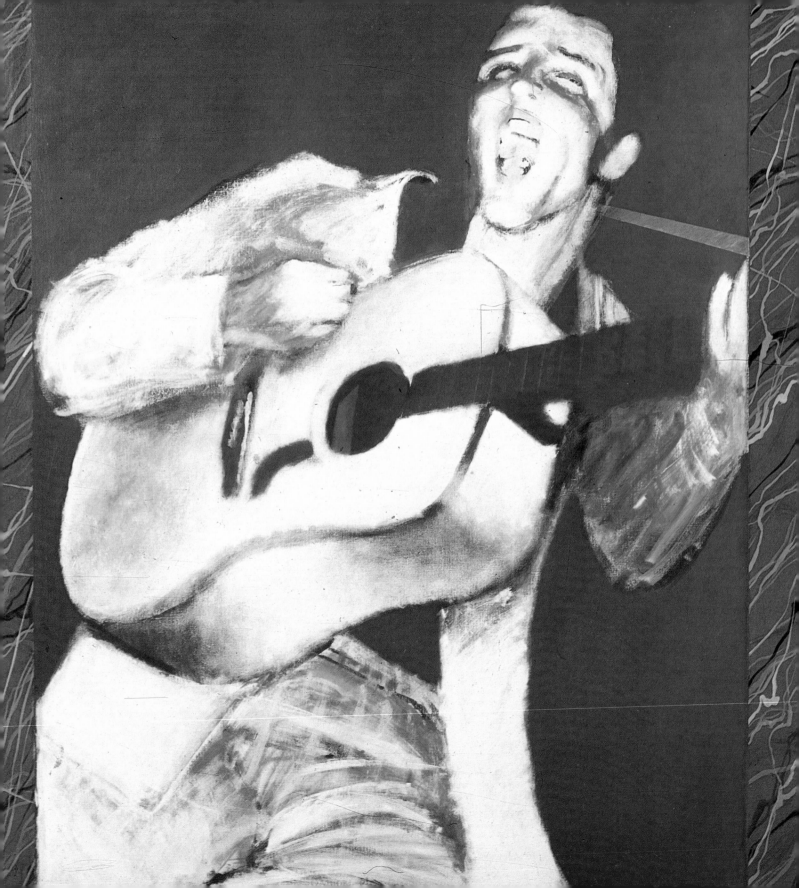